STICK YOUR HEAD UNDER THE SURFACE

by

Bruce Muench, Aquatic Biologist

Roscoe, Illinois

Photographs by Author

Best wishes,
Bruce
Muench

Second Printing
ISBN: 0-9659221-0-3
Copyright © 1997 by Bruce Muench
6918 Saladino
Roscoe, Illinois

Warning—Disclaimer

This book is designed to provide information in regard to the subject matter covered. It is sold with the understanding that the author is not engaged in either promoting or criticizing any product mentioned herein.

It is not the purpose of this book to reprint all the information that is otherwise available to the author. There may be mistakes, both typographical and in content. This book contains information only up to the printing date.

The purpose of this book is to educate and entertain. The author will have neither liability nor responsibility to any person or entity with respect to any loss or damage caused, directly or indirectly, by the information contained in this book.

If you do not wish to be bound by the above, you may return this book to the author for a full refund.

Acknowledgments

There are many people I should thank for helping me during the writing of this book, but surely as God made little, green apples I'll remember some of them only after this book comes back in final print. For that, I pray your forgiveness.

Most of all I should thank my wife, Dorothy, who allowed me to mess up one whole room of the house for several years with my "necessary" papers strewn all over the place. Also, we had frequent arguments with regard to respecting my "space" while in the throes of writing and she allowed these tantrums without taking me too seriously.

I need to thank my kids, especially sons Kevin and Peter, who helped with various phases of the pond management and investigation when it became more than I could handle myself. Other members of the family helped too.

Without help from friends who edited various chapters, you the reader would encounter much more fuzzy sentence structure, misuse of punctuation and misspelling of words than you will find. Special thanks must go to Keith and Jeanette Kratz, Dr. William Howenstine, and to Evelyn Robinson.

Advice was also given by people like James Mayhew, retired head of the Fish Section of the Iowa Department of Natural Resources and by Darlene Fiske, an Audubon-type person, for her review of my waterfowl chapter. Also, Bill Piper kindly flew me in his plane around our farm in order that I could take some aerial photos. Dax Kirchhoff, an artist and another family friend, did most of the black and white drawings found in the text.

Finally, thanks to all those like Bob and Marcia Parker who supported me morally and actually believed that I would finish this book, even though my faith in the project would wax and wane almost as frequently as the phases of the moon.

The Basis of This Book

It seems that I was always interested in water. Maybe it started with liking the aquatic environment of my mother's womb too much. As a boy I was fascinated by all kinds of water, from the polluted Des Plaines River nearby, to even a mud puddle where algae was growing. This preoccupation with water later led to my joining the U. S. Navy and ultimately to my occupation as an aquatic biologist.

In my professional life, I have been involved with the investigation of many hundreds of different bodies of water such as lakes, ponds, streams, and rivers. Most of my work has been in Illinois and the majority of that has been with small lakes and ponds. Illinois has at present, 80,000 bodies of water which could be classified as ponds, and although no two bodies of water are the same, they are akin in certain climatic and biological ways. The most common category of these small bodies of water is the farm pond.

When I first felt an impulse to put down on paper my experiences as a biologist, it seemed impractical to discuss the whole kaleidoscope of waters with which I have worked. As you will see, I chose instead to write about our own farm pond and deal with that in detail. Hopefully, this makes a more interesting and personal story.

Discussions with pond and lake owners, those who live near bodies of water and people just interested in aquatic biology, lead me to believe there is very little in the literature to which they can relate, one on one. Certainly, what is available in our scientific journals has poor relevancy to them. My wish is that the reader of this book will come away with a new appreciation for the natural and not-so-natural events that can happen to our surface water resources, and also perhaps with some of the feeling of mystery that I have, when after nearly fifty years of being immersed in the subject, both literally and figuratively, feeling a little overwhelmed by the different world of the aquatic environment.

List of Charts, Maps, Graphs and Tables, in Order

	Title	Chapter
Figure D.	Depth contours of pond	Construction
Figure T.	Transparency of water	Water Transparency
Figure N.	Pond stratification	Stratifications
Figure S.	Sediment in pond	Sedimentation
Figure X.	Some features of pond	Dissolved Oxygen
Figure L.	Pond location in midwest	Winter conditions
Figure PS.	Seasons of plants	Aquatic plants
Figure C.	Herbicide chemicals	Aquatic plants
Figure W.	Bird sightings by month	Waterfowl
Figure G.	Great blue heron	Waterfowl
Figure F.	Time-line of fish species	Fish
Figure Y.	Bass and bluegill growth	Fish

List of Pictures

Figure number	Heading	Chapter
Cover	Farm and pond	Cover of book
Figure 1 A	Scraped pond basin	Construction
Figure 1 B	Shape of pond	Construction
Figure 2	Kids sitting on discharge pipe	Looking back
Figure 3	Field erosion	Watershed improv.
Figure 4	Grass waterway	Grass waterway
Figure 5	Bio-logs	Other measures
Figure 6	High water overflow	Water levels
Figure 7	Low pond level	Water levels
Figs. 7 B,C,D	Four months of low water	Water levels
Figure 8	Secchi disc	Transparency
Figure 9	Organic sediment	Sedimentation
Figure 10	Exposed pond bottom	Sedimentation
Figure 11	My canoe	Water chemistry
Figure 12	Dissolved oxygen test	Dissolved oxygen
Figure 13	Venturi aerator	Aeration
Figure 14	1/2 h.p. compressor	Aeration

Figure 15	Bricks weight air line	Aeration
Figure 16	Aerator hole in ice	Aeration
Figure 17	Aerator line tubing	Aeration
Figure 18	Taping air line	Aeration
Figure 19	White alum floculant	Phosphorus mgmt.
Figure 20	D-Phos A	Phosphorus mgmt.
Figure 21	Pond winter scene	Winter conditions
Figure 22	Ice skating party	Winter conditions
Figure 23	Steve fell through ice	Winter conditions
Figure 24	Ice rink cleared of snow	Winter conditions
Figure 25	Winterkill of fish	Winterkill
Figure 26	Sterile bacteria bottle	Bacteria
Figure 27	Chara	Aquatic plants
Figure 28	Filamentous algae	Aquatic plants
Figure 29	Kids swimming	Aquatic plants
Figure 30	Leafy pondweed	Aquatic plants
Figure 31	Illinois pondweed	Aquatic plants
Figure 32	Cattail leaves	Aquatic plants
Figure 33	Cattail tuber	Aquatic plants
Figure 34	Fiber-mesh sheeting	Aquatic plants
Figure 35	Water buttercup in bloom	Aquatic plants
Figure 36	Liverwort	Aquatic plants
Figure 36 B	Bulrushes	Aquatic plants
Figure 37	Purple loosestrife	Aquatic plants
Figure 38	Grass carp stocking	Grass carp
Figure 38 B	Dead grass carp	Grass carp
Figure 39	Adult dragonfly	Insects
Figure 39 B	Dragonfly nymph	Insects
Figure 40	Snail and clam	Insects
Figure 41	Cornfield above pond	Pesticide kill
Figure 42	Pesticide fish kill	Pesticide kill
Figure 43	Pick up dead fish	Herbicide kill
Figure 44	Snapping turtle	Reptiles, etc.
Figure 44 B	Leopard frog	Reptiles, etc.
Figure 45	Bullfrog	Reptiles, etc.
Figure 46	Two species of tadpoles	Reptiles, etc.
Figure 47	Baby raccoon at night	Other animals

Figure 48	Son with deer	Other animals
Figure 50	Nesting box in pond	Waterfowl
Figure 51	Ducks Unlimited nesting box	Waterfowl
Figure 52	Wood duck in tree	Waterfowl
Figure 53	Screech owl in D.U. box	Waterfowl
Figure 54	Hole in channel catfish	Waterfowl
Figure 55	Redwing blackbird	Waterfowl
Figure 56	Redwing nest and eggs	Waterfowl
Figure 57	Crayfish	Fish
Figure 58	Stocking small bass & bluegill	Fish
Figure 59	Six inch one-year-old bass	Fish
Figure 60	Bluegill spawning nest	Fish
Figure 61	Nine-inch bluegill	Fish
Figure 62	Cloverleaf fish trap	Fish

Contents

Preface
  Acknowledgements iii
  Basis of This Book iv

I. How It All Began
  History of Land Use 1
    Setting for Pond and Planning 3
    Construction of Pond 4
    Looking Back 8
  Watershed 11
    Pond Filling 12
    Physical Improvements 12
    Grass Waterway 13
    Other Pond Measures 14

II. Physical Things Happening to Pond
  Water Levels 17
  Stratification of Water 19
  Water Transparency 21
  Sediment and Sedimentation 31

III. Chemical Things Happening to Pond
  Water Chemistry 36
  Dissolved Oxygen 39
    Aeration and Aerators 45
  Alkalinity and pH 57
  Phosphorus 59
    Phosphorus Management 62
  IBI and TSI 75
  Nitrogen 78

IV. **Seasonal Things Happening to Pond**
Winter Conditions 81
    Ice Cover 82
    Other Winter Conditions 87
Winterkill 88

V. **Biological Things Happening to Pond**
Bacteria 94
Aquatic Plants and Their Control 97
    Generalities 116
    Grass Carp 118
Insects 123
Pesticide Fish Kill 126
Herbicide Fish Kill 130

VI. **Animals In and Around the Pond**
Reptiles and Amphibians 140
Warmblooded Animals 142
Waterfowl 153
Fish, Mainly Largemouth Bass and Bluegills 165
    Smallmouth Bass 177
    Northern Pike 179
    Channel Catfish 183
    Trout 184

VII. **Epilogue**
Things You Can Learn from a Pond 187

Chapter 1

History of Land Use

Background and history

After completing school in the mid '50s, my wife Dorothy and I decided not to return to my hometown of Des Plaines, Illinois but to look somewhere "out in the country" for a place to live. The Des Plaines of my boyhood was no longer the relaxed, small town of vacant lots and leisurely traffic and people who actually walked from one place to another. Des Plaines had become, for better or worse, part of the suburban sprawl surrounding Chicago.

Our search ended after four months in southwestern McHenry County, about sixty miles northwest of Chicago, at a 160 acre grain/dairy farm. My father, a pharmacist in Des Plaines most of his life, was helping us search for a home. He was approaching retirement, as was the farmer (Mr. Fritz) whose property had so much appeal to both Dad and me. The farmstead had two houses—the old, larger original farm house and a newer, smaller frame house where Mr. Fritz's son, Bob, lived with his family.

So it came to pass that in 1958, my wife and I and our three young children moved onto the farm and Mr. & Mrs. Fritz and their son's family moved into the nearby small town of Marengo—a kind of cultural exchange that has been going on for the past forty years in this part of the country. Unfortunately, nowadays, the exchange more often involves the farm being lost to land development interests and ending up in small lot subdivisions; hence farms are lost permanently to agricultural production.

The Fritz's had been farming here since about 1900. At some time around the turn of the century, about thirty acres of oak savanna woodland had been cleared off the south end of the place, leaving about thirty acres of woodland remaining intact at the time we purchased the land. It was within this remaining woodland that we found the most likely site to build a pond.

In American Indian times, which means prior to 1840 in this neck of the woods, the vegetation here was oak savanna in the uplands and prairie openings or wetlands in the flatlands. This can still be determined from the soil types we find on the farm, with Miami and Drummer soil associations reflecting predominantly woodland and prairie origins respectively. The Potawatomi Indians, the last of the tribes to live here prior to white man's influx in the 1830's, were hunters and gatherers and did a little farming. I doubt that they did much to modify the character of the land, although they probably set some fires in their pursuit of either clearing land or hunting. My two sons, Kevin and Peter, have found numbers of Indian artifacts on the farm such as projectile points and stone chips (lithics). They seem to occur at concentrated locations on the property, perhaps reflecting old campsites. Until around 1850, when immigrants began clearing off the woodlands and plowing the soil, this land did not greatly change.

Farming in this area by more recent settlers was primarily a dairy, hay, pasture and cash grain effort from 1860 to 1960. The same was true of Mr. Fritz's farm, where he maintained a herd of around forty-five dairy stock. Dairy farming was generally favorable to the quality of the cultivated land because hay and small grain fields, necessary feed for dairy cattle, were usually rotated through the cropland fields, along with corn and later soybeans. Also, much animal manure was hauled out to the fields in the cleaning of barns, barnyards and animal sheds. This organic material was plowed and disced into the upper soil of the crop fields prior to the next planting season, providing both a boost in fertility, in addition to maintaining the tilth of the soil, by incorporating this organic material with the inorganic soil particles.

The death knell of dairy farming in McHenry County has been brought about by the labor-intensive nature of milking, the need for expensive modernization of milking methods and facilities, and the increased value of farmland as a commodity for sale to housing developers and land speculators. Today, improved highways and transport trucks have made it possible for dairy farmers to be located far up into Wisconsin and still be able to service the Chicago market or "milk-shed" area.

Following World War II, with the decline of local dairying, came an increase in cash grain, row-crop farming. Most farm lands which had once been used for pasture, hay and small grains, were converted to intensive cultivation for corn and soybeans. No longer was crop rotation being practiced as a normal course of farming and no longer were large quantities of nutrients and organic material being returned to the soil in the form of animal manure. One has only to take a leisurely drive through our county for an hour or two to see all the empty silos, large barns, hog houses and chicken coops, to appreciate what has been happening in the changing farm scene. When we purchased the Fritz farm in 1957, there were twelve active dairy farms within a mile-and-a-half radius. In 1995, only two remain, and one of these may not survive the next five years.

Setting for the Pond and Planning

Back about the time Jesus was telling Simon Peter and Andrew to throw their nets on the other side of the boat, there were lots of ponds in this part of the midwest. Mostly these bodies of water were a gift of the last glacier that receeded back to the north some 13,000 years ago, but a few were leftover bends of rivers that decided to change course. Some of these glacial-made ponds are still around, many of which are now wet spots in the corn fields where farmers get stuck with their tractors in the springtime. There are three such wet spots in our cultivated fields and two more in our woods. The two in the woods are about a half-acre each in size and nearly grown over with cattails.

In our woodlot, there was actually a better site for building a new pond than would have been presented by digging out those old, natural depressions. In the era of the '60s, the U. S. Department of Agriculture, through its county Agricultural Conservation Program Service, offered cost-sharing for building fish ponds, or livestock water ponds, built on farmland. The site for the pond and the practicability of construction first had to be approved by a technician. In this instance, the technical expertise was provided by the U. S. Soil Conservation Service, located at the county seat of Woodstock. The two S.C.S. technicians for our county, Sam Haning and Clayton Bruce, had much experience with pond construction practices, having designed a great number since this popular conservation practice began. The degree of cost-sharing was determined mainly by the extent of earth-moving that needed to be done.

Clayton Bruce, an affable and efficient S.C.S. man, came out to look over two possible pond sites in April of 1963. He selected an upper location in the woodland, which was the beginning of a small tributary. I helped him survey the area by holding a stadia rod, while he sighted through the transit, setting topographic contours of the land for every foot variation in level. Clayton had just one hand, by the way, which appeared to be only slight handicap to his activities. He calculated that it would require moving about 7,000 cubic yards of earth to construct a pond the size (about two acres) and depth (maximum nine feet) that would be suitable, From other topographic maps, Clayton knew there was from 40 to 45 acres of land above the pond site that would drain into it. This is the watershed which would provide, through rainfall runoff, the primary water supply for the pond. Most of this runoff could be anticipated from snow-melt and from heavy rains in May and June, when little land vegetative cover would be present. This is the same time of the year when the sump pumps in people's basements can be expected to be running.

Besides a water supply, what is needed for a pond which is impounded by a dam is a good, tight subsoil on the bottom and in the dam. This prevents leakage when the water becomes impounded. Clayton and I made a number of test soil borings in the proposed pond basin and along the dam site and found the soil the be mainly a suitable clay loam. The soil which was to be excavated from the basin would be used to build the dam.

Construction of the Pond

Talking about the construction of the pond may not be the most interesting part of this book, but I figure I have to *get* the pond born, before I write about what things happen on and to it.

In the summer of 1963, I solicited bids from four local companies that had some experience in pond construction. Two of the four eventually submitted actual bids. The less experienced of the two submitted the lower bid, which was $0.30 per cubic yard to move the 7,000 cubic yards for the basin and to construct the dam. The other bid was $0.35 per cubic yard. Were the same bid to be made in 1996, the cost would probably be closer to $3.00 per cubic yard.

The procedure followed in the actual construction, which was accomplished in a ten-day span in July of 1963, was as follows:

1. The four mature oak trees which stood where the pond and dam were to be built were knocked down with a bulldozer and stacked out of the way to the south of the site. Incidentally, these trees were still useable as firewood some twenty years later.

2. The topsoil was scraped with a turn-a-pull and bulldozer from the basin of the pond site and stockpiled to one side.

3. The dam location was scraped down to clay, and a core trench about four feet wide and four feet deep, excavated along the length of the dam site.

4. The turn-a-pull scraped soil off the pond basin (Figure 1 A), then dumped and spread it while driving parallel along the dam site. A bulldozer follows to compact and level the soil with its caterpillar treads and blade.

5. After completion of the earthmoving, the top soil which had been stockpiled, was graded on top of the dam and on the down-slope side with a bulldozer, to a depth of about one foot.

6. The overflow pipes I had ordered and which had been delivered prior to earthmoving, were put into place by cutting through the center of the dam fill to its base. A concrete platform was poured in the pond side and the 36-inch diameter riser pipe placed upright on the platform. The 24inch diameter tube was laid through the dam and connected to the bottom of the riser.

7. Two metal anti-seep collars, or diaphragms, six feet square in total, were placed and welded to the 24-inch pipe passing through the dam at about the midway point. These were installed

to prevent seepage along the outside of this pipe once the pond was full. All the pipes and the seepage collar were copper-steel, corrugated, galvanized and were bituminous-coated. Most of the bituminous coating on the exposed pipes was not evident 15 years later.

8. A parallel 1-1/4 inch diameter iron pipe was also placed through the dam about twenty inches below the level of the top of the riser, and about ten feet to one side of it. This was designed to allow us to draw water by gravity from the pond by means of opening a valve on the other side of the dam. On the pond side, this pipe elbowed into a steel drum filled with rock that sat on the pond bottom. The rock would hopefully act as a coarse filter for the water being drawn out of the pond. One of our thoughts was to water cattle below the dam and while they were fenced off from entering the pond itself.

Within three weeks after completion of the earthmoving, I seeded the soil on top of the dam and wherever else topsoil had been placed. The object was to stabilize the soil with new vegetation and to prevent subsequent erosion. The seeding utilized was primarily oats, alsike clover, fescue, and perennial grass, which was planted with a grain drill. The Soil Conservation Service had recommended the type of seeding to be used. This seeding became quickly established, and the perennial grasses and some of the clover are still present thirty-some years later.

We completely fenced off the pond from the pasture prior to releasing cattle and horses into the pasture. The objective of this was to prevent hoof damage to the dam, but also to avoid fecal contamination and extra nutrients from entering the pond.

The shape of the pond ended up looking like a kidney bean (Figure 1B), with a small peninsula about 70 feet in length and 45 feet wide, jutting out into it from the east. Part of the reason for the peninsula was an attempt to save two mature bur oak trees from being bulldozed into oblivion and also to provide a more interesting and diverse shape to the shoreline. Unfortunately, the oak trees did eventually die about four years after the pond filled.

The actual size of the surface water area ended up at slightly over two acres when the pond is full to capacity. Maximum depth is 9-1/2 feet in an area of about 1/2 acre where the greatest excavation took place. The remainder of the pond basin is from two to five feet deep (Figure D). Subsequent years demonstrated that

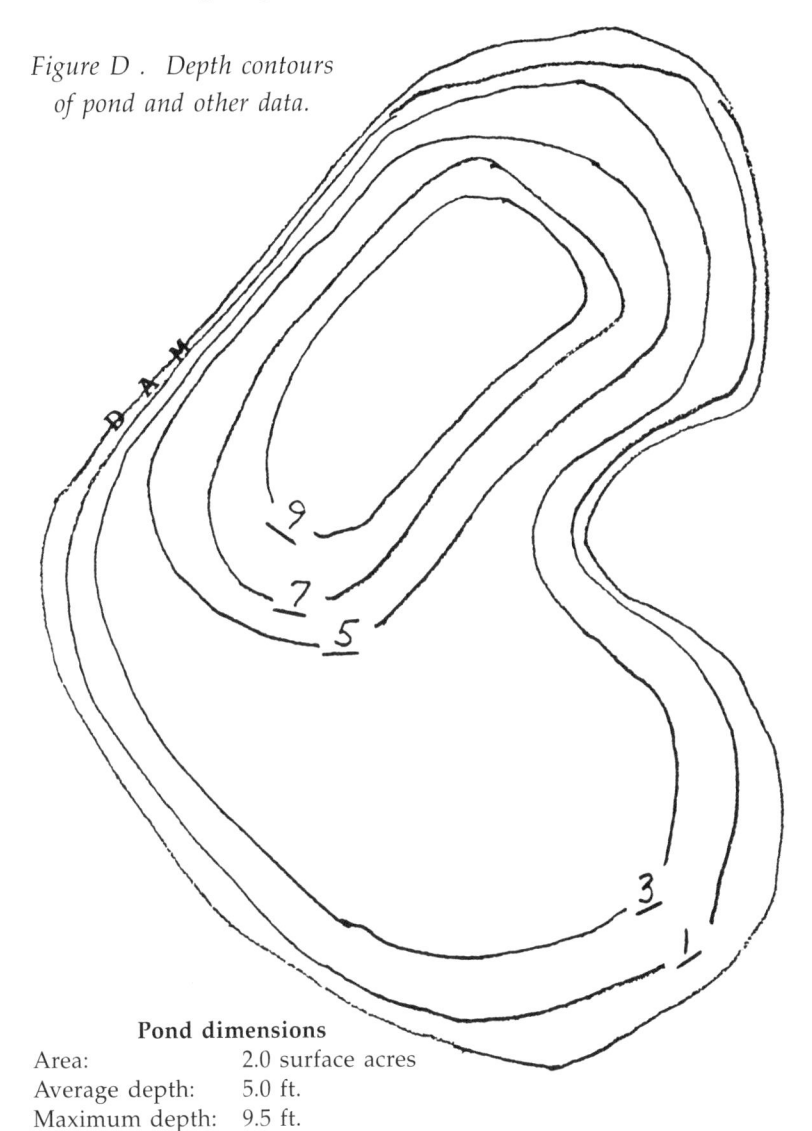

Figure D. Depth contours of pond and other data.

Pond dimensions
Area: 2.0 surface acres
Average depth: 5.0 ft.
Maximum depth: 9.5 ft.
Volume: 401,000 cu. ft.
Watershed: 40 acres

all areas of the pond which were less than eight feet deep, were subject to growth of rooted, submergent aquatic plants.

The pond is located 650 feet south of our farm house, making it convenient to walk to, but remote enough not to be seen from the house and nor by yard activities to frighten any animals that may be using the pond. The exception to the "availability" of the pond from the house is in winters when snow may accumulate to a depth of more than three feet. This has happened a couple of times in the past. I solved this problem somewhat with the purchase of a snow plow attachment to my four-wheel drive truck in 1985. Now I can plow my way from the house all the way around the pond, and when necessary, plow snow off the surface of the pond itself.

Looking back

With thirty-plus years of experience following the construction of the pond, I can look back on some of the things we did right or wrong in its initial construction.

First, in letting out the bids for construction, I should have looked more carefully at the previous pond work done by the two bidders. If I had, I would probably have chosen the higher bidder, who had much more experience and who had constructed some excellent ponds within thirty miles of ours. The bidder I chose, although competent, did not excavate the pond bottom to the shape and depth that I had prescribed, resulting in years of aquatic weed problems that were worse than they would have been had the pond been deeper.

Part of the blame for this I must accept myself. I was not present during most of the actual construction, being off in Canada fishing with my oldest son. Possibly, if I had been on-site daily I could have had the contractor correct what I consider now to be inadequate excavation. I did say something to him about this a month after construction was completed, but he made no effort to either acknowledge or correct the situation.

My attempt to save some of the oak trees near the water met with mixed results. The two trees on the peninsula died, as I said previously. Also, most of the oak trees on the immediate shoreline of the pond died within five years after the pond filled, probably from having their roots in ground which was now saturated with water. Oddly enough, some of the oak trees which were situated a little further back from the pond's edge, more than twenty feet, still survive today, although off and on, they may have had a sickly look. Long-term survival probably depends upon how much of their shallow root system was injured during construction, and how much of their root system ended up in saturated soil.

For such large trees, oaks, like the bur oak and white oak which predominate on our place, have relatively shallow root systems. Knocking these trees over with a bulldozer was surprisingly easy. I observed. If one wished to save oak trees around a new pond being constructed, I would suggest forgetting about those quite close to the water and take them down right away. As for those further back, first fence the area so heavy construction equipment cannot run underneath their canopy, and then do not allow new earth to be piled or graded underneath the trees. Also, do not attempt to establish grass seeding under the trees unless using shade-tolerant varieties. At my pond, oak reproduction in the form of young trees, has now grown up quite near the pond where the older trees died out. No doubt the young trees have sent their root system to such a depth that they are not into the water-saturated soil. Some of the young bur oak trees are now twenty feet tall.

The U.S. Department of Agriculture cost-share practice for fish ponds, under which we obtained assistance for constructing our pond, is no longer offered in Illinois. In McHenry County, this practice ended in 1980, although there continues to be programs available for shallow, wildlife ponds and for stock watering ponds on a low-priority basis. One of the reasons for eliminating the fish pond practice was ostensibly because many ponds were constructed in existing wetland areas, which have unique values in and of themselves. This would disregard the fact that the majority of such ponds were located in areas where they would be creating new wetlands and expanded aquatic habitat for many plants and animals. They also serve as mini-reservoirs which help to "level-off" flood runoff peaks, recharge ground water tables, and remove sediment from surface runoff waters.

Because of moist conditions in August, after I seeded the dam and earthen fill areas, a healthy growth of vegetation followed. This cover helped to prevent soil erosion from occurring which could have been detrimental to the steeply-sloping surfaces on both sides of the dam. Had washing of soil become a problem here, I could have secured fiber mesh and straw matting on the surfaces and seeded directly into these materials. Erosion on newly scalped or filled, sloping earthen surfaces can be quite serious. Establishing grass seeding, or temporary mulch covers, can prevent erosion and the subsequent need for costly reshaping of exposed surfaces. Fortunately, in the instance of my pond, there were no heavy rainfall events following construction and until vegetative cover was established.

The oversize spillway and discharge pipes used in the pond design proved their worth in later years (Figure 2). Only three times has the water level risen more than 18 inches above the spillway riser outlet and been diverted through the emergency spillway over one shoulder of the dam. As a consequence, the dam has never been damaged by flood waters. Also, the 24-inch diameter tube through the dam is large enough so I could crawl inside it to fix a leaky internal joint of two sections of the pipe within the dam.

Placing the anti-seep collars on the tube passing through the dam also proved its worth. Within seven years after construction, muskrats were burrowing into the face of the dam. Muskrats tried to follow the outside of the tube through the dam, but were thwarted, fortunately, when they encountered the large, metal anti-seep collars attached at right angles to it. There is not much water pressure on the dam, even when the pond is full, because only about five feet of water column is actually impounded against the face of the dam. The dam itself is quite thick, with a ten-foot minimum width roadway along the top, and about 50-foot-width at its base; consequently I have never had leakage through the dam itself. However, there is some seepage through the base of the dam, probably through the sub-surface. This seepage is minor, but has been present ever since water has been impounded, and the amount of seepage has remained essentially the same for over thirty years. Most dams do develop wet areas below their downstream faces. In mine, willows and other wetland plants have occupied this area to the extent of about 1/2 acre. A similar wetland area has developed in the drainage way immediately *above* the pond, where soils also have become saturated by the raising of the original ground water levels. Both of these new "wetlands" have some attraction to wildlife, and are occupied with various species of wetland plants, such as willows, cattails, sedges and beggars tick.

Watershed

The water supply for most ponds in the midwest comes from rainfall which drains off the surface of the land that is above the pond itself. This upper land which drains into the pond is called its "watershed". It might be likened to a baby's bib in that all the food and drippings that baby drops, hopefully, will end up in the pouch at the bottom of the bib. In this instance the bib is the watershed and the pond is the pouch.

The watershed which leads to our pond is 40 acres in size, almost entirely located on our farm. In this part of the country, where average annual rainfall is about 33 inches, it is considered that from 15 to 25 acres of watershed is sufficient to maintain one surface acre of pond water. It would appear therefore, that our pond is in pretty good balance with its watershed at a 20:1 ratio (40 acres watershed to a two surface acre pond). Before the pond was built, this watershed land was mostly in row crops, such as corn and soybeans, although a little also drained off from a neighboring woods and our own woodland.

Because the soils in the watershed land have much clay, the rainfall runoff tended to be rapid. This, coupled with the fact that there was also a cultivated hillside in the drainage area, means that during heavy rainfall soils may be eroded by runoff water, soils which could end up in the pond. This could create conditions where the pond may fill rapidly with sediment.

Pond filling

After the pond construction was completed on August 1, 1963, it required seventeen months of rainfall runoff to fill and overflow the spillway riser for the first time. The cumulative amount of precipitation which had fallen at a U.S Weather Bureau station three miles away, was 45 inches during this time interval. This could be considered about "average" rainfall for this area, according to Weather Bureau records. This means that the "catchment" period, or "retention" time for the pond is about 17 months. In other words, this is the time required for the pond to completely replace its water volume once.

Knowledge of the time required for a pond to fill with water under normal rainfall conditions, is important in several respects. It allows one to calculate an annual budget for determining any particular nutrient inflow and residence time in a body of water. It also offers information about the period of time for refilling the pond when drought may lower the water level, or when the pond needs to be drained and refilled for some management purpose.

The yield of runoff from rainfall in any watershed varies according to the time of year, vegetative cover, slope of the land and intensity of the precipitation. For example, a one-inch rainfall in mid-July spread over a twelve-hour period, would not yield nearly the water flow to the pond that a one-inch rainfall in late March over a two hour period would yield. Both intensity of rain and lack of ground cover in the March example would accelerate runoff.

Pond and watershed physical improvements

Within the pond's watershed is one hillside of about five acres with a slope of from 4% to 7%. At the time of pond construction this hillside was being cultivated, and gully and rill erosion were evident along the steeper areas. The worst of the gullies were knee deep.

In 1958, five years before the pond was built, I decided to

use a soil conservation measure on the hillside to prevent erosion. In the spring, we purchased 500 jack pines and 500 red pines from the State Department of Conservation and planted these seedling trees on about one acre of the hillside, spacing them on six foot centers. My object was to not only take this land out of cultivation, but to provide some eventual wildlife cover, and perhaps use it for Christmas tree production. In subsequent years, I planted the four remaining acres of the hillside with more Christmas trees, using mainly scotch and white pines. Success of survival of the seedling pine trees varied considerably from year to year—anywhere from 85% to 15% survival to the next year. Survival hinged most upon how moist the soil conditions were in the immediate summer after planting, and also the following summer. Usually, if the trees made it the first two years they were able to survive long-term.

Annual and perennial plants grew up with the Christmas trees and offered considerable ground cover. The areas which had sheet erosion and gullies could hardly be distinguished when walking over them ten years after planting. I would guess that reducing the erosion on this hillside, along with installing a subsequent grass waterway, greatly reduced the potential sedimentation in our pond after it was built. Field erosion is evident in Figure 3.

Grass waterway

Ten years after the pond was built, I asked the U.S. Soil Conservation Service of McHenry County to design a grass waterway in the watershed immediately above the pond and leading into it. The waterway designed by their Soil Conservationist, Greg Waggoner, in October of that year, was 1500 feet in length, and accommodated a change in gradient from 5% at the upper end (fairly steep) to 0.3% close to the pond (pretty flat). The channel varied from 30 to 48 feet in width. This grass waterway was constructed in June of 1976. Seeding of oats, timothy and red fescue was drilled in the landscaped earth in early August by the man who was renting our farmland, using a seeding formula provided by the Soil Conservation Service. Weather conditions were ideal during the construction and seeding of the grass waterway, and subsequently a good germination of grasses followed. Growth was encouraged with an application of 1,000 pounds of 12-12-12 fertilizer. I spread a straw mulch over the exposed soil the next day following seeding. Almost no heavy rainfall runoff occurred for two months following. Twenty years later, a very good cover of fescue is still present in this waterway, and almost no erosion or gullying has occurred within its designed boundaries (Figure 4).

It has been estimated for McHenry County, that installation of a grass waterway will save in its lifetime an average of four tons of soil for every 100 feet of waterway. Using such a ratio, a 1500 foot waterway would save 60 tons of sediment to my pond during the lifetime of the waterway. In its twentieth year thus far, I am certainly pleased at the manner in which it has held up.

Other Pond Measures

Another source of erosion i.e., that caused by wave action, became evident along the face of the dam within two years after construction. This was before a good grass cover had become established on the slopes of the dam. In order to diminish the effect of the wave action, I decided in 1966 to use some stone to riprap the inside dam face at about the level the water would be when the riser was overflowing. For this purpose, I utilized field stone, which was glacial rock that was removed by the farmer each spring from his cultivated fields in an effort to protect his plowing, discing and planting tools. He had established a rock pile of about 30 ft. by 30 ft. by 5 feet high in the wooded pasture near the pond, an accumulation of rock from many years. Some of this rock was also used in the construction of the base of several of our farm buildings. I find myself still using this stone pile thirty years later, and it continues to be replenished each spring by stones which heave up out of the cultivated fields.

I transport the stone in the front-end scoop of my tractor and place them by hand wherever I can see wave erosion. The average stone is about head-sized. This is not a one-time job, unfortunately, as the stones move by gravity and the kids like throwing them into deep water. I get to enjoy the job of refurbishing this stone riprap (that's the proper word), nearly every year.

I transported the rock in the front end scoop of a tractor to various spots along the length of the dam, and hand-placed each stone in a two-tier deep line. It was easy to tell where the stone should go, as a noticeable erosion depression had developed by this time at the normal water level. The average stone could best be described as between double-fist and head-sized. I have refurbished the stone riprap over the years by replacing it with other stone or broken concrete from the neighbor's old patio. Because it is usually flat on at least one side, the broken concrete seems to stay in place better, but is not as pleasing or natural to view.

More recently I have begun the installation and testing of a shoreline protection product named "Bio-log". This consists of a burlap-wrapped cylinder or roll of coconut fiber. These rolls are placed parallel along the shoreline wherever one wishes to prevent wave erosion, and are staked down with oak stakes every four feet (Figure 5). The rolls also can be inoculated with the seeds of water tolerant vegetation. The seeds may germinate when moist and will not only root the Bio-log to the bank, but will cover it with natural-looking vegetation. We got our Bio-logs from Randy Stowe, a biologist who specializes in erosion control and lives at nearby Harvard, Illinois.

The rest of the shoreline around the pond has not shown the effects of erosion, so it has never been necessary to protect it anywhere other than on the dam. Some minor damage has been done by burrowing muskrats elsewhere, but mostly their activity has been aimed at the inside face of the dam, where they burrow just under the water line, and come up inside the dam to make a den which is both enclosed and above the water line. In narrower dams, muskrats can cause considerable damage, including water leakage through the dam, and caving in of the top of the dam.

In February of 1969, I could hear some water leaking inside the tube passing through the dam. When I got down inside the riser, (the pond was not overflowing), I could see leakage in the joint between the tube and the riser pipe. Ground frost had apparently heaved up the lower (outside) end of the tube and caused a slight separation in the joint with the riser. Of course, the riser could not move because it is seated in concrete. Water seepage through this leak was not great, perhaps twenty gallons per minute. After the frost went out of the ground a few days later, the tube apparently realigned itself and the leakage stopped.

The following year, in February, the same thing happened. This time the leakage lasted longer, and after about ten days I decided to do something about it, fearing that it might become worse. Fortunately, I don't suffer from claustrophobia, so I crawled into the tube, and where the two pipes join, I pressed some lead wool into the open joint with a screwdriver. This lessened the seepage considerably, and after a few more days it stopped. I haven't experienced serious leakage through this pipe joint since, and assume that the dam fill and the pipes have now settled into place in proper alignment.

Chapter 2

Physical Things Happening to Pond

Water Levels

Since 1965, I've kept a record of the water level of the pond. I do this by measuring the vertical difference between the existing water surface level and the top edge of the riser spillway. Many times, of course, the water would be going over the top of this vertical spill pipe, and I would then record the level as "full". The percentage of time the pond has been full in different months for the past 30 years is below:

Month	% of time pond is full
January	59
February	63
March	81
April	84
May	74
June	38
July	8
August	19
September	15
October	17
November	17
December	46

I can say for my pond that for January through May, it is usually full, while from June to November, it is usually not full. The lowest water level I've recorded thus far was in August of 1971, when the level measured 65 inches below the spillway. At that time, there was only four feet of water remaining in the pond basin. Five months of drought preceded this measurement and the farm crops were withering in the fields.

The water level is not only dependent upon the amount of rainfall runoff, but also upon the rate of evaporation and transpiration from the pond itself. It appears that the rates of evaporation and transpiration are nearly double in August from what they are in October. The water temperature averages about 70°F in August, but only 50° in October. Perhaps of equal importance, growth and transpiration of nearby aquatic plants, such as cattails which surround the pond, are much more vigorous in midsummer than in October.

Runoff from the watershed into the pond becomes more reduced when the ground is covered with growing plants. During the ten years that 25% of the watershed was in conservation reserve grasses, coupled with another 20% of the watershed in pine trees which I had also planted, it became quite noticeable that the rainfall runoff from May to October was considerably restricted. This was due to the greater evaporation and transpiration caused by the added growth of ground cover. During the cold months, when most of these plants are dead, rainfall runoff is much more efficient, and pond water levels hold higher. Frozen soils tend to accelerate melt-water runoff.

There have also been periods of very high water levels, almost always in the spring, and usually in April. This is before sufficient ground cover plants have grown over the watershed, which would slow down surface runoff water. In April of 1972, the year following the drought of '71, pond levels reached a record high of nearly two feet above the spillway riser pipe (Figure 6). When the level gets to be over 17 inches above this spillway, the water begins to overflow an emergency, grass spillway, which is a seven foot wide low spot in the south shoulder of the dam. This prevents it from washing over the top of the dam and causing erosion. In 30 years, the water level has been high enough to go over this emergency spillway only three different times; however, it paid for itself the first time it happened in the protection to the dam it afforded. Accompanying these high water levels and rapid runoff is usually high turbidity, or muddiness in the water. This will be discussed in another section.

When the water level remains low and exposes some of the original pond bottom during the warmer months, terrestrial plants quickly begin to colonize the exposed wet and drying soil

(Figure 7). Plants like smartweed may grow as high as three feet before the pond area they are growing in becomes reflooded (Figures 7 B, C, and D). Birds take advantage of the seeds of these plants, if the plants are given time to mature.

During the period that pond soils are drying, large cracks usually appear in its surface. On rare occasions, I have been able to drive a tractor over this exposed surface, and have also been able to get a tractor stuck in it, much to my family's amusement.

Stratification of Water

When I talk of water "stratification", I refer mainly to two water quality parameters, dissolved oxygen and temperature. The changes in water quality can be great from the surface of a pond or lake to its bottom, especially if that body of water is deep and especially during warm weather. However, if you hear someone say that these water measurements do not also change in a shallow body of water, like my nine foot deep pond, as I said before, tell them "Baloney!"

In the warm months (June to September), there are usually two or three "layers" of water in the pond: (1.) A top layer of warmer water, usually fairly high in dissolved oxygen; (2.) A middle layer of water where the temperature is dropping, as is dissolved oxygen; and sometimes (3.) A bottom layer where water is consistently cooler and dissolved oxygen is almost always low, or entirely absent (Figure N). These individual layers may range from three to five feet in thickness. Presence of turbid water, whether due to plankton algae or to sediment in suspension, tends to give more distinction to each layer.

Layering of dissolved oxygen, but not temperature, may exist under the ice in the winter. The position of low dissolved oxygen will start at the bottom in the deepest water, and will extend further upward in the water column with time, particularly if a heavy snow layer persists on the ice. Temperature differential under the ice in the pond does not vary any more than five or six degrees Fahrenheit (32-38°F) with the warmer water near the bottom.

Figure N. Typical pond circulation and stratification.

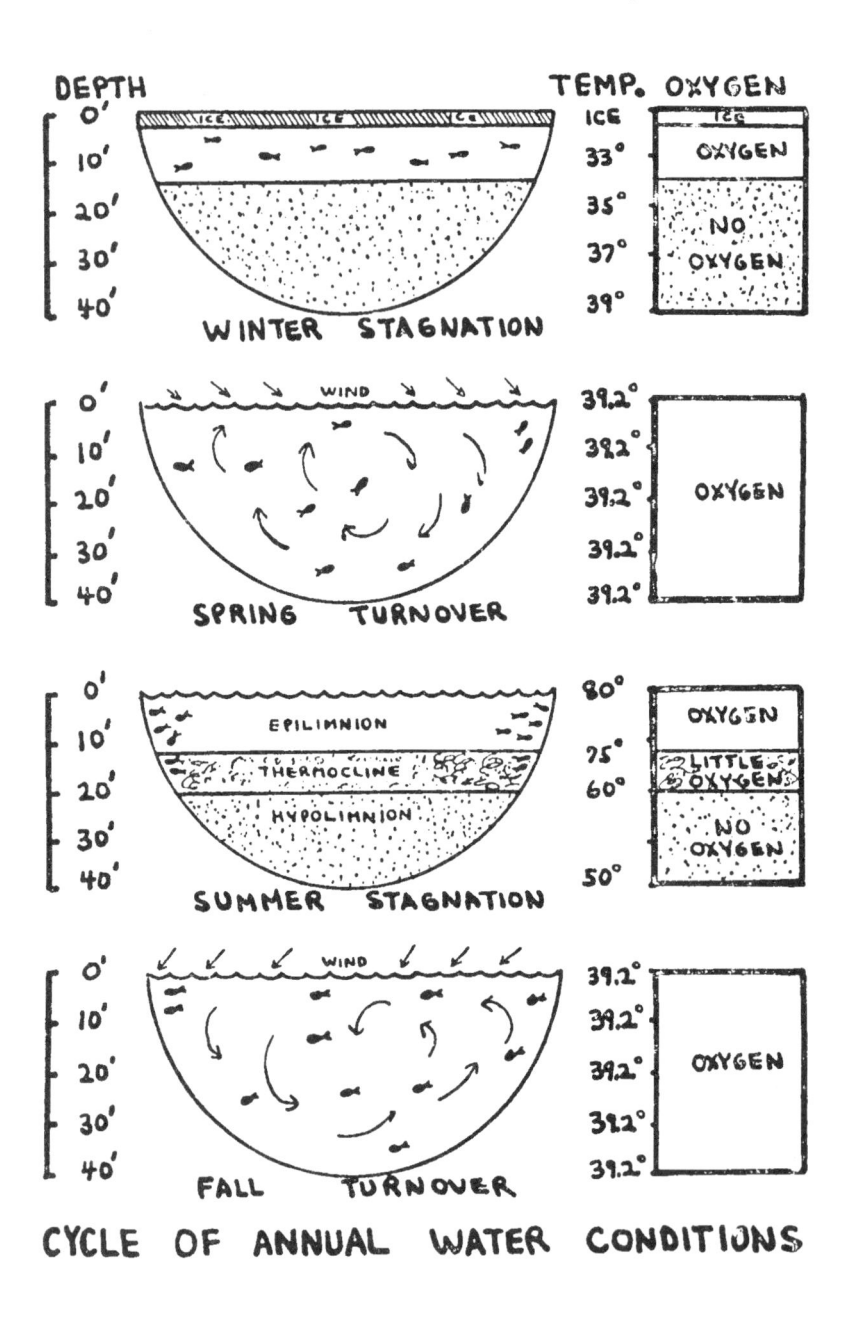

CYCLE OF ANNUAL WATER CONDITIONS

Water Transparency and Turbidity

Transparency of water generally refers to how far one can see down through the water column. This may be expressed in inches of visibility. Turbidity, although directly related to transparency, refers more often to the amount of suspended particles in the water column, and is usually expressed in quantities of milligrams/liter. I have conducted both kinds of measurements in the pond, making hundreds of measures of transparency using a secchi disc, but fewer laboratory measurements of turbidity. Consequently, the discussion below relates mainly the transparency information and how it effects life in the water.

Aquatic biologists generally agree that clear water is more productive for most kinds of sight-feeding fish and aquatic life than muddy water. In fact, clear water (visibility over thirty inches), may be five times more productive for bass and bluegills than water with a visibility of only five or six inches. Growth of both bass and bluegills is also more rapid in clearer water. Fishery people like to see at least nineteen inches of transparency in a body of water with these two species of fish present.

One measures the transparency by lowering a black and white secchi disc into the water (Figure 8). Where the secchi disc goes out of sight is measured in vertical inches as transparency. This is the depth at which approximately 95% of the sunlight has been eliminated by shading from particles in the water column. A small fraction of the light can penetrate to almost three times this depth.

Figure T shows the average transparency of the water in our pond, by month, for the past twenty-four years. Although average transparency was always better than nineteen inches per month, in actuality, 20% of the time individual measurements were *under* nineteen inches, or less than desirable for fish like bass and bluegills. Most of the muddy water was encountered in March and April, following spring snow melts and heavy rainfall runoff from a relatively unprotected watershed. Poor transparency from May through September was more often the result of the strong presence of plankton algae. Sometimes during muddy water runoff in March and April, visibility was as poor as four to ten

Figure T. Average Transparency (inches) of Pond Water by Month (1966-95).

·········· minimum desirable for fish

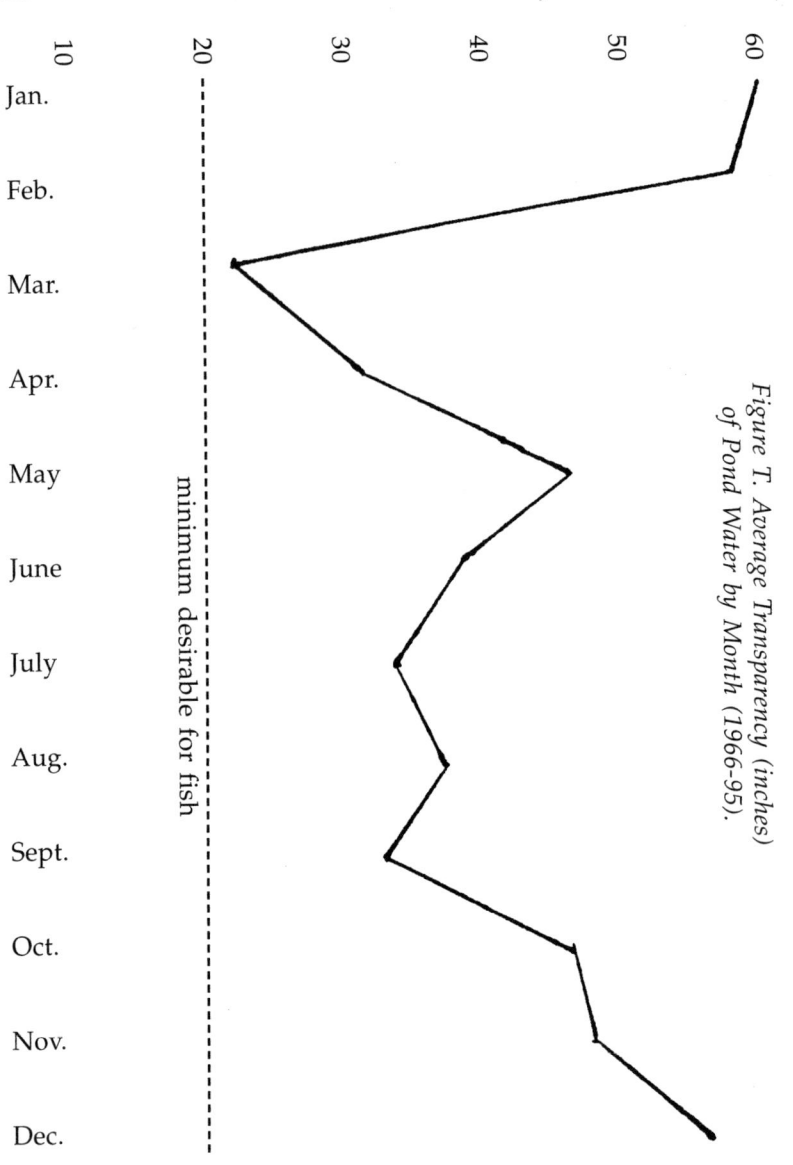

inches, with the water having a clay color. From May to September, visibility rarely was under eleven inches, and the water color at those times when it was less was bright green.

Presence of both rooted, submergent and emergent aquatic plants, during the warm months, tends to settle out soil particles

Figure 1A. Scraped pond basin.

Figure 1B. The pond shape 9/25/67.

Figure 2. Pond overflow after cloudburst of Spring '65.

Figure 3. Run-off water from field to pond.

Figure 4. Pond watershed 8/24/92.

Figure 5. Bio-logs of two sizes in the pond.

Figure 6. Riser of pond overflowing after heavy 3" April rain.

Figure 7. Exposed pond bottom, October '88 drought.

*Figure 7B.
2 months
exposed.*

*Figure 7C.
3 months
exposed.*

*Figure 7D.
4 months
exposed.*

Figure 8. Secchi disc.

Figure 9. Organic sediment.

Figure 10. Plants growing on dry bottom.

Figure 11. My canoe.

Figure 16. Aerator hole in ice.

Figure 17. Aerator line bubbling.

which may wash into the pond. In times of high turbidity, one can usually find clearer water amid the cattails along the shoreline compared to that further out in the pond. Heavy growth of submergent aquatic plants, like water buttercup and chara, tends to settle out suspended soil particles quickly. This is mainly a result of the plants presenting a barrier to water movement.

Two management measures which were undertaken that could help account for clearer pond water since 1975, are the construction of a grass waterway within the watershed leading to the pond, in June of 1976, and the treatment of the pond itself with aluminum sulfate, in June of 1984. These management measures are discussed in more detail elsewhere.

Because sunlight is essential to aquatic plant growth, just as it is to plants on land, the depth to which water plants can grow is directly related to water transparency. Taking an average transparency and multiplying by two will give the effective depth of sunlight stimulus to plants. In other words, if transparency in May averages four feet, aquatic plants in my pond get enough light to grow to a depth of seven or eight feet. Deeper than that, there would be no rooted plant growth on the bottom. Even under the ice, if sunlight can penetrate the ice and snow, some submergent plant species may continue to live and to produce oxygen. I have taken oxygen tests under the ice in midwinter when it was clear, and found super-saturation (a surplus) of dissolved oxygen to be present.

Besides all of these good, biological reasons for having clear water, there is the fact that clear water just *looks* better to people. This is true whether one is interested in swimming, fishing, or boating in it, or maybe just having a picnic next to it. The only aquatic organisms in my pond that may not care whether the water is clear or not are the channel catfish and perhaps the crayfish. This is because these animals can still feed effectively by sense of feel or smell, even though the visibility is poor.

Sediment and Sedimentation

As ponds and lakes get older, they tend to have "gunk", or sediment, accumulate as bottom deposits (Figure 9). This material may be organic, like dead aquatic plants and leaves, or it may be inorganic, like soil particles which have washed into the basin. The rate of accumulation of these sediments may offer a clue to the useful life of the body of water, that is, when it becomes so shallow that it becomes more a wetland than an open body of water.

As you might suspect, this rate of filling-in is rarely regular, like 1% per year. The rate of filling depends both upon the extent of erosion occurring in the watershed, along with the immediate shore and also upon the amount of organic material which is deposited each year.

In our pond, during its first ten years, most of the sediment accumulation was inorganic soil which had washed in off the farm fields above it. This happened particularly at times of heavy rainfall runoff. Once I had covered the steeper slopes with grasses and trees and had developed the grass waterway in 1976, leading into the pond, the soil sedimentation decreased markedly. After 1977, the sediment which has accumulated has been mostly organic and comes from dead aquatic and wetland plants, plus leaf-fall from trees near the pond.

I didn't begin making accurate sediment measurements in the pond until nearly 20 years after it was built. In the past twelve years (1983-95), I've made six different mappings of sediment measurements (Figure S).

To measure sediment on the pond bottom, I used a steel rod which has depth markings along its length. If the pond is nearly full of water, I measure from a boat at periodic intervals along three pre-arranged pathways transversing the length and width. I let the rod down to where I can first feel it touch resistance, and record this to the surface of the water as "water depth". Then I push the rod down until I meet firm resistance of the original pond bottom, which was clay, and measure this difference as "inches of sediment thickness". This method, although somewhat subjective, is satisfactory for me as long as I use the same methodology each time.

What have I found out in my pond over the years? I found that most of the sediment had accumulated in the first 18 years

Figure S. Pond with 5 foot depth contour

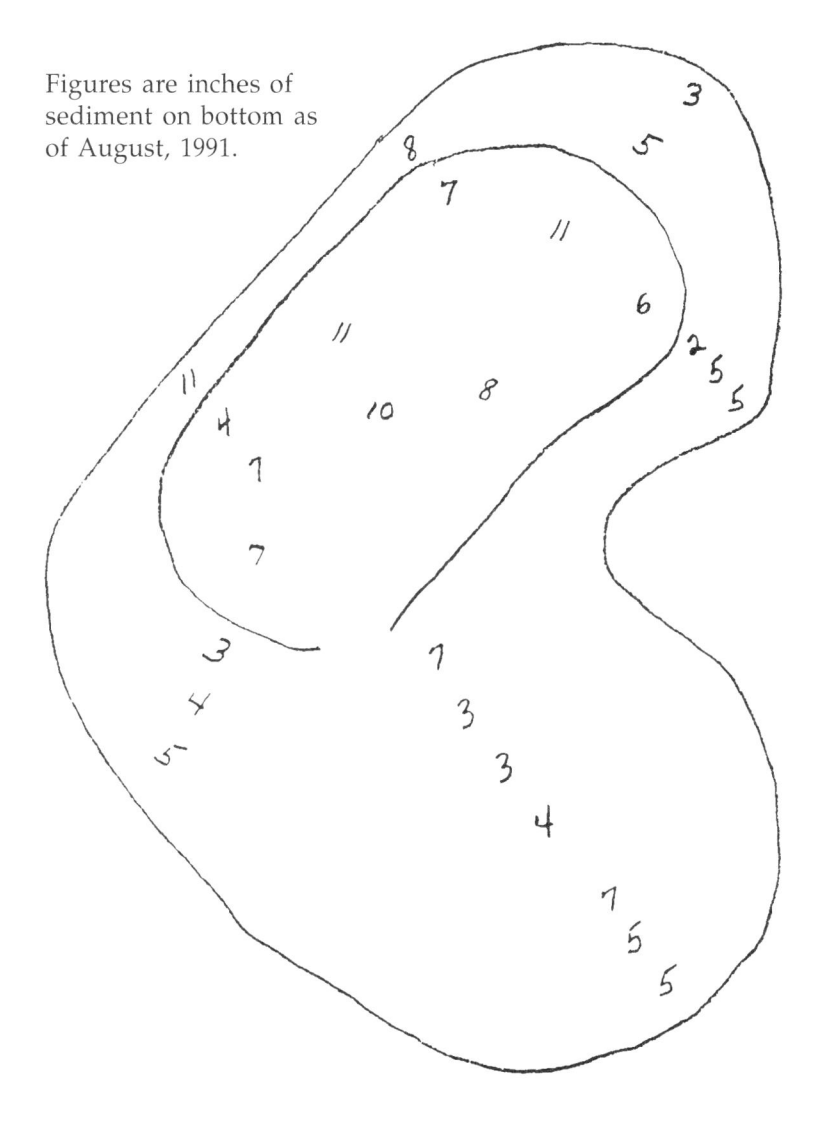

Figures are inches of sediment on bottom as of August, 1991.

of the pond's life, and that the sedimentation rate after that has been quite slow and has consisted mostly of deposits of dead organic material. I can tell the difference between the organic material and the inorganic in two ways: (1.) The organic stuff is usually grey or black in color, while the inorganic is clay color, more brownish, and (2.) The organic material smells a lot and the inorganic doesn't. When I pull the measuring rod out of the sediment, it's fairly easy to tell one from the other.

One factor tends to confuse the issue when measuring sediment in the shallow part of the pond. During low water periods, when the pond bottom is exposed to the air for several weeks, the exposed sediment shrinks and cracks. When this exposed part of the pond becomes re-flooded, the sediment does not swell back up to its original size, but remains shrunken. As a consequence, one may measure the sediment thickness in shallow water one year, and three years later, find it to be less, due to an intervening period of exposure to the air. Sediment in the deeper part of the pond, which is never subject to drying, does not do this.

Also, the sediment which becomes exposed to the air loses much of its organic content, due to the more rapid and complete oxidation process which it experiences. It also tends to lose its blackish color on its surface, unlike the deep water sediment which remains black and stinky. Lately I've been moving my operating aerator line over to different locations in deep water, hoping to better oxidize the organic sediment. So far it doesn't seem as if I'm getting any significant results, but maybe I haven't tried it long enough.

Back to the sediment measurements which I have taken in the pond. In 1996, which is present time, the sediment measures from 3-12 inches in thickness in deep water, averaging 7.1 inches. In shallow water, sediment measures from 2-11 inches thick and averages 4.8 inches. Variation in sediment thickness can be great from spot to spot. In 1983, I measured 24 inches of sediment, mainly inorganic, just 15 feet out into the lake from where the tile water enters. This was a small delta of soil that had entered with the tile water and got blown out further into the pond before it got a chance to settle out. Sediment in this same location three years later, measured only seven inches.

It appears that in the thirty year life span of our pond, there has been a loss of approximately 10% of its water volume, due to sedimentation (Figure S). The nice thing is that the rate of sedimentation is decreasing now. The sad thing is that now most of the sediment is organic in nature, which is of more negative impact in terms of water quality, principally in its effect of lessening dissolved oxygen. The organic sediment also tends to be rich in nutrients, like phosphorus, which may in turn stimulate other plant growth like luxuriant amounts of algae. This has been a general trend in my pond for the past twenty years, that is, more organic sediment and more algae.

The exposure of expanses of the pond bottom to air during prolonged periods of low water, brings another biological factor. Besides the exposed bottom mud becoming cracked during dehydration, terrestrial plants begin to grow voluntarily after a period of time. Indeed, after a period of three months of drying, these plants may virtually cover the exposed bottom (Figure 10). Plants most likely to appear conspicuously are nearby moist-land species, such as water smartweed with its pink-colored flowers in the summer, bur-reeds and sedges. These plants have value as food for wildlife and especially for ducks when the pond bottom becomes flooded once again.

Chapter 3
Chemical Things Happening to Pond
Water Chemistry

Spring, Summer and Fall

Since 1967, I have conducted some kind of water chemistry test or another on about 300 different days. The distribution of the tests in different months is skewed somewhat toward the summer and also toward January, because these usually were the critical periods of water quality.

On test days, almost always a vertical depth series of dissolved oxygen and water temperature was taken. Occasionally, tests were taken at two or more locations in the pond on a given day, and sometimes tests were taken every eight hours through a continuous 24 hour night/day series. Frequently, the pH of the surface water was measured, and sometimes tests for total phosphorus, nitrate nitrogen, ammonia nitrogen, total suspended solids, and volatile suspended solids were taken. Also, water transparency was measured even more frequently than dissolved oxygen.

Methods of water examination used included:

Dissolved oxygen: Either rapid Winkler chemical method, a Hydrolab, or a Sentry III (made by Otterbine) electrical meter.

Temperature: Either a mercury thermometer, or a Sentry III meter.

pH: Rascher/Betzold color comparitor.

Water transparency: Secchi disc.

Total coliform and fecal coliform bacteria, Total alkalinity, Total phosphorus, nitrate, nitrite and ammonia nitrogen, volatile and total suspended solids: Standard methods for water examination at National Environmental Testing (NET) Laboratories in Bartlett, Illinois. References for methodology include: 1. "Methods for Chemical Analysis of Water and Wastes", UKSEPA, 600/4-79-020, Rev. 1983, and 2. "Standard Methods for the Examination of Water and Wastewater, 17th Ed., APHA, 1989.

Samples were taken to this lab, in the bottles provided, within two hours following collection. Other methods of sample preservation, such as cooling and use of preservatives, were also followed.

Infrequent tests were also taken for orthophosphate, Kjeldahl nitrogen, specific conductance, methyl orange alkalinity, sulfate, chloride and silica. Examination of these parameters were usually conducted at NET Laboratories, the commercial testing lab mentioned above.

Many dissolved oxygen and temperature tests were taken to compare water chemistry with the aerator system running, and with it shut off for varying lengths of time. Tests were also performed to compare "before" and "after" water quality, when certain other management measures were undertaken, such as phosphorus reduction and aquatic plant control. Tests were conducted to compare conditions of prolonged drought and sudden flooding. Pesticide examinations of pond sediment were made in May of 1987, following a die-off of fish at that time. Most, but not all, of these samples were also examined at NET Laboratories.

The costs of some of the tests and the testing equipment which I commonly used on the pond, follow:

	Approximate Cost in 1995
Otterbine Sentry III, electric oxygen and temperature meter	$360.00
Mercury thermometer	26.00
Fisher pH color comparitor kit	80.00
Secchi disc (Wildco Supply Co.)	51.00
Kemmerer plastic water sampler closing bottle	250.00

Laboratory costs (per test):

Immunoassay test for four common pesticides	150.00
Total coliform bacteria	10.00
Fecal coliform bacteria	15.00
Total alkalinity	10.00
Total phosphorus	25.00
Nitrate/nitrite nitrogen	25.00
Ammonia nitrogen	30.00
Volatile suspended solids	15.00
Total suspended solids	10.00

I used my canoe most of the time to take the water tests out in the pond (Figure 11). The canoe is left near the pond all year long, upside down. When using it, I paddle it out to my sampling location and anchor it there. Because the canoe is aluminum, it has held up quite well over the twenty years I've had it. Only once have I accidentally tipped it over. Occasionally I will use my 14-foot jon boat with its outboard motor to take water tests. Because it is very wide in the beam, I have yet to be able to turn it over even though I sometimes sit on the edge of it. With a canoe one needs to be much more careful and one had best be a good swimmer before fooling around in it. The axiom applies: "If you canoe, expect to swim".

Surface water or ground water flow can sometimes contaminate well water, especially if the well is relatively shallow—like less than fifty feet deep. If a person is interested in testing the quality of water in a rural drinking water well, one often can get this service from the County Soil and Water Conservation District or the County Department of Health where he or she lives. Their contracted service may include testing the water for volatile organic chemicals, including agricultural pesticides, and a variety of metals. This is especially important to have done in shallow wells and old wells. It is also important in agricultural areas which are rapidly becoming urbanized. I began testing our own well water in 1993, and will continue to do so each year, even though nothing suspicious has shown up as yet. Probably the most important examinations of well water would include the various coliform bacteria tests, and tests for nitrate nitrogen. On these two parameters, there are state health regulations as to what is safe for drinking water.

Many of the sample results which are listed in the text of this book are shown as "mg/L", which means the concentration of the substance in units of milligrams per Liter of water. For example, I may state the concentration of oxygen in water to be "9.5 mg/L". This also can be expressed as parts "per million" (ppm), which is equivalent.

Dissolved Oxygen

On over 500 occasions during the life of the pond, I have conducted dissolved oxygen tests of the water. This was done because oxygen is such an essential part to life in water, just as it is on land. Usually a test consisted of a series of measurements, perhaps for each foot of vertical depth in the water column. Almost always, water temperature was also measured at the same depth.

The usual sampling location was over the deepest water (Figure X), but frequently, tests were also taken in shallow water for comparison. In some instances, tests were taken every eight hours for a 24-hour night/day series.

The two principal sources of dissolved oxygen in pond water are solubility of oxygen gas in surface water which is in direct contact with the air, and production of oxygen by algae and other aquatic plants through photosynthesis within the pond. Photosynthesis is the food making process of green plants. In respiration, green plants take in oxygen and give off carbon dioxide, just as we do in breathing; however, in photosynthesis, the same plants take in carbon dioxide and give off oxygen. They do this when in the presence of sufficient sunlight. It may take only 15% of full sunlight to enable the plants to start photosynthesis, thus they can do so on cloudy days, or underneath an ice cover.

The solubility of oxygen in the water varies with the water temperature, i.e. the colder the water, the more oxygen it can hold. For example, water can hold twice as much oxygen at 32°F

Figure X. Some features of the pond.

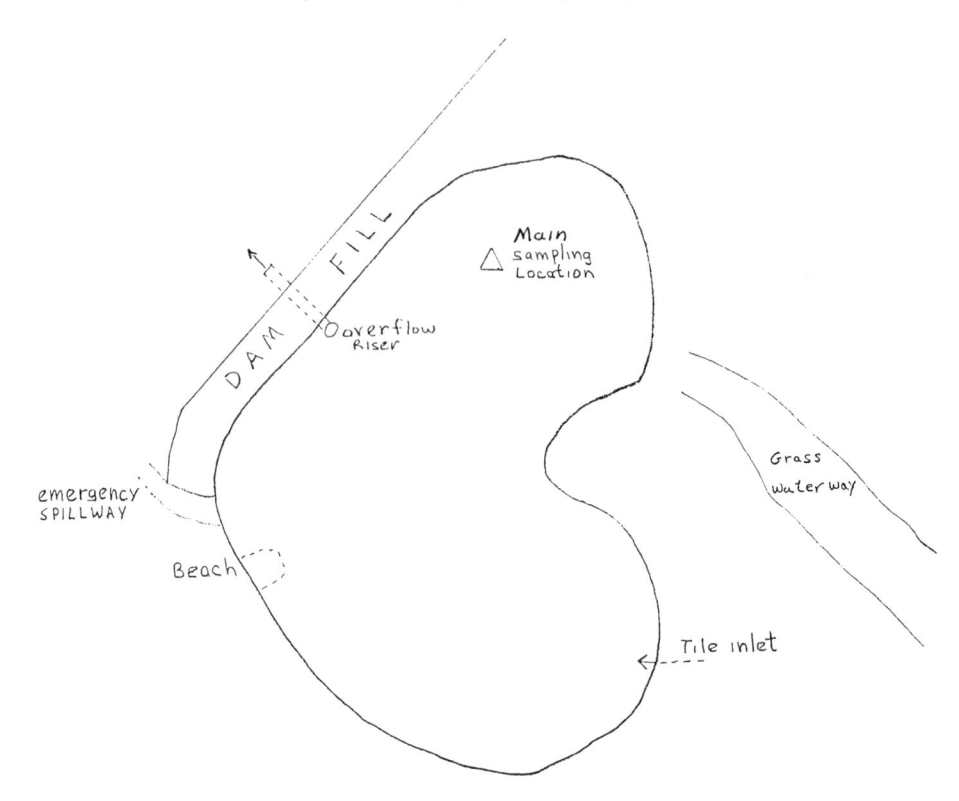

as it can at 88°F. There are times when water may hold *more* oxygen than it is supposed to. This usually will occur under the ice, when the ice is clear and the day is bright and sunny. At such times the water may be "supersaturated". I have observed this on several occasions in my pond . . . at which times there may be 130% or more dissolved oxygen for a given water temperature. For example, on March 11, 1995, with seven inches of clear ice and no snow cover on a bright day, the dissolved oxygen tested over 16 mg/L at a depth of three feet. I also took, at the same time, a test of the water coming into the pond from a field drain tile. This tested 8.5 mg/L. Obviously, the water picked up dissolved oxygen while residing in the pond. In the pond, photosynthesis was occurring as a result of a complete blanket of green, filamentous algae which covered the bottom everywhere less than eight feet deep. The ice cover was acting as a lid over the surface to prevent excess dissolved oxygen from escaping to the atmosphere, like the cap on a coke bottle.

During a prolonged dark period, dissolved oxygen becomes depleted, the extent depending upon how long the light is absent. Fortunately, there is usually enough oxygen produced during the day to carry the aquatic animals easily through the dark nighttime periods.

Excessive production of dissolved oxygen can also be associated with the supersaturation of another gas, nitrogen, which can cause gas bubble disease in fish, when nitrogen emerges from the blood stream and may lodge as bubbles under the skin or in the fin membranes. I first observed this in bluegills in January of 1968. The dissolved oxygen was 16 mg/L at the time. I did not measure the nitrogen level, but it also had to be high. Use of the aeration system in the pond can sometimes relieve this situation of supersaturation.

Because dissolved oxygen in water is so essential for all kinds of aquatic life, most aquatic organisms begin to suffer when the oxygen content gets lower than 3 mg/L. There are some water organisms, such as midges, that can get along for awhile with very little or no dissolved oxygen, but they are in the minority. Usually when dissolved oxygen is lacking, other gases which may be toxic, such as carbon dioxide and hydrogen sulfide, become more prevalent. Some species of fish, such as bullheads and northern pike, can also get along on less dissolved oxygen than bass and bluegills.

I have encountered low dissolved oxygen conditions in the pond in the summer and late winter, but almost never in the spring or fall. In midsummer, when water temperatures are typically "layered", i.e. warm on top and cold on bottom, the water in the bottom layer may contain less than 4 mg/L dissolved oxygen (see Chapter on Stratification). Because of the difference in density between the warm and cold water layers, little mixing is possible by wind action, and this stagnation condition may remain the same for as long as two months. This is not always true, for perhaps 30% of the summers there was ample oxygen from the surface to the bottom. Whether this condition occurs depends much on water clarity, extent of plant growth, wind and wave action, temperatures, and also upon whether the aquatic plants are healthy or dying. However, when water temperatures are about the same from top to bottom, as in the spring and fall, the water and the dissolved oxygen become well mixed.

Often when photosynthesis by algae is occurring at a rapid rate during bright, sunlit days, the bubbles from excess oxygen may float or "balloon" the algae up to the surface, where it forms scummy mats. This happens in my pond particularly when filamentous algae is abundant. On those occasions when I have taken dissolved oxygen tests during warm weather at intervals of eight hours over a 14-hour period, the following results are typically obtained (D.O. = Dissolved Oxygen):

At 3 p.m., D.O.= 8.8 mg/L, at 10 p.m., D.O.= 8.2 mg/L, at 5 a.m., D.O.= 4.6 mg/L.

In this instance, I am using the test depth of three feet; however the same trend is evident in all depths. By mid-afternoon, the production of dissolved oxygen by plants has just about reached its peak level, and consequently D.O. levels are high in the water column. Even at 10 p.m., there is still ample dissolved oxygen left from the daytime photosynthesis, even though it has now been dark for two hours. However, by 5 a.m. the next morning, the dissolved oxygen has become depleted, or used up, to the extent where only about half is left from the mid-day high. After a few hours of morning sunlight have passed, dissolved oxygen will begin rising rapidly. This is the living response of plants to stimulus of sunlight.

On one occasion in August, the dissolved oxygen became so low that most of the fish suffocated. At this time, dissolved oxygen concentrations were below 4 mg/L throughout the water column for ten days. This was complicated by a prior treatment of aquatic plants with a herbicide, bringing about excessive decomposition (see Herbicide Fish Kill section). There have also been two winters when dissolved oxygen became so low as to kill fish (see Chapter on Winterkill).

When fish suffocate in the summer because of low dissolved oxygen, most frequently, the large individual fish will die before the smaller ones of the same species. I noticed this particularly in July of 1995, when it appeared that most of the adult bass and bluegills were floating dead at the surface, while all the small juveniles of each species were still actively swimming around in water with less than 2 mg/L dissolved oxygen. One would be led to believe that there is a differential requirement for dissolved oxygen for maintaining life between small and large individuals, indeed I think this is true. In the summer, die-off of fish is more likely to occur late at night, or early in the morning. Again, this is because the aquatic plants have lost the benefit of sunlight for producing oxygen and are instead in a state of using up dissolved oxygen and producing carbon dioxide and other gases.

When I would test similar depths at two or more locations at the same time for dissolved oxygen, I would usually get about the same dissolved oxygen values. However, when plants were dying, I would sometimes get significantly lower dissolved oxygen in shallow water, where the plants were located, than in deeper water where plants were absent. This suggests there is a localized depletion of dissolved oxygen caused by the decomposing plants. The greater the amount of plant growth in a lake or pond, the more the impact of photosynthesis and respiration; so in shallow ponds like mine, there is great influence. Taking dissolved oxygen tests at two separate locations over deep water at the same time through the ice revealed slight differences at the same depths, but not much.

One February 5th, I tested dissolved oxygen and pH of surface snow-melt water, which was entering the pond through the inlet, tile and also water which was going out over the spillway. The snow-melt water had a dissolved oxygen (D.O.) content of 12.5 mg/L and a pH of 6.6, the incoming tile water a D.O. of 9.6 mg/L and pH 6.9, and the water going out over the spillway, a D.O. of 8.0 and pH of 7.0. In this instance, the water running into the pond from snow melt and through the tile, was recharging the dissolved oxygen in the pond. Also, the pH of this water was becoming more alkaline by virtue of its passing through the captured elements in the pond. I suspect that this is a typical situation when much snow melt runs off into any body of water.

During some winters, when snow would persist for a long time on the pond's ice cover, I would shovel off strips of snow, down to the surface of the ice. By doing this, I hoped to increase the ability of sunlight to penetrate through the ice, and to stimulate aquatic plants to continue to produce oxygen through photosynthesis. This was somewhat frustrating at times because the snow would frequently blow back over my plowed strips and I would need to shovel again and again. (Who needs an exercycle?) I also don't know how much of the area of the surface (10% or 50%) I would need to clear to provide meaningful light stimulus to the plants, but I do know that if the plants are *completely* shaded by snow cover for long enough, they will die.

One of the methods of measuring dissolved oxygen in water is called the "rapid Winkler method". This involves using various amounts of chemicals, one of which is sulfuric acid. The reader may appreciate by the accompanying photo (Figure 12) that I sometimes spill a little acid on my work coat, which my wife, Dorothy, has mended several times. More frequently, I measure with an electrical meter both dissolved oxygen and temperature, much to my wife's relief.

*Figure 12.
Dissolved oxygen test.*

Aerators and Aeration

I got my main "push" for providing artificial aeration to the pond from having two successive, partial winterkills of fish during the winters of 1976-'77 and 1977-'78. "Winterkill" is the suffocation of fish and other aquatic animals under the ice after prolonged reduction of dissolved oxygen in the water, usually to a level of less than 3 mg/L. Contributing factors include: (1.) Long term, heavy snow and ice cover, blocking the sunlight into the water necessary for plant life photosynthesis and, (2.) Organic decomposition taking place in the pond under the ice, albeit at a slow rate, which further uses up available oxygen. The first winterkill did not occur until the pond was thirteen years old.

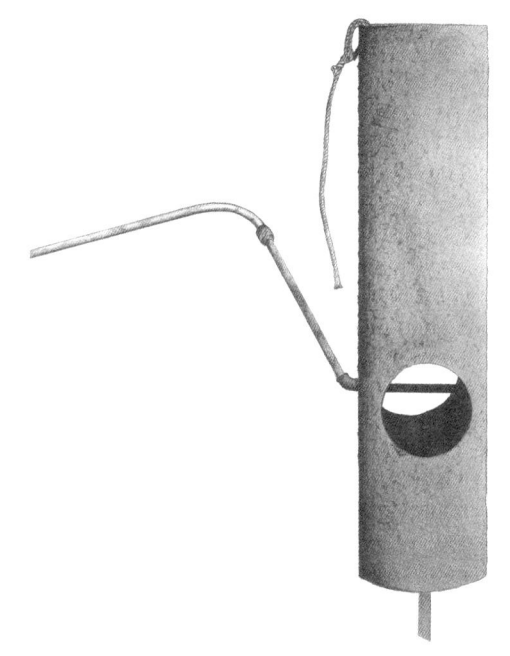

Figure 13. Venturi aerator tube.

In October of 1978, I installed a venturi-type aerator (Figure 13) in the middle of the deeper, nine foot part of the pond. This device is designed to circulate large volumes of water by having air bubbles rising from the bottom up to the surface in a vertical, circular flow. This essentially equalizes dissolved oxygen and other water quality parameters over a large portion of the pond. For example, instead of having 1 mg/L of dissolved oxygen near the bottom and 10 mg/L at the surface with no circulation, one may find 5 mg/L throughout the water column *with* the venturi operating. The term "destratifier" may be more appropriate for this kind of water circulation device, than "aerator", as it is problematic concerning how much additional dissolved oxygen may be entering the water by exposing it to the surface air.

The compressor which supplied the air to the venturi was a 1/2 h.p., oil-less, 115 volt unit (Figure 14), which John Fitzpatrick and I mounted on a wooden post about fifty feet away from the pond's edge. We ran a underground, waterproof, electric cable, which was buried one foot deep, from the barn to the compressor. I have had no trouble with this cable in the sixteen years since it was installed. The whole system cost me about $700.00.

From the compressor, a 1/2 inch diameter, plastic tube runs

Figure 14. 1/2 h.p. compressor.

out into the pond and to the venturi. To keep this air line on the bottom, I strapped building bricks, two every ten feet, to the tube (Figure 15). I made the mistake of crimping this plastic line accidentally when I first laid it out, and later it leaked air at this weakened point. I then had to replace the tubing.

Figure 15. Brick strapped to air tube.

The venturi has a pointed steel stake on the lower end, and this is shoved into the pond's bottom, so it stands upright. Occasionally it has fallen over, but it is not difficult to reposition. When the compressor is running, the bubble disturbance at the surface of the pond is about twelve feet in diameter. The actual area of circulation influence is much greater than this, as I have observed underwater, using SCUBA. I would estimate the total area of influence to be at least sixty feet in radius.

This first type of aerator I operated, off and on, from late 1978 through 1982. In that period, I conducted dissolved oxygen tests on 43 different dates, and made comparisons of the effects of the aerator on dissolved oxygen when it was operating and when it was off, for varying lengths of time, sometimes for a complete year. I also made several comparisons of how long it took the aerator circulation to break through ice cover, once it was started.

During this period of 4-1/2 years, the system developed four failures. Once the air hose had a hole shot through it by my son-in-law while he was target practicing behind the dam. Another time, small ants got into both the compressor and the air line, reducing its efficiency by about 50%. A third instance, the bearings wore out on the motor after 3-1/2 years. The fourth was the ants again, when they plugged up the electrical outlet to the compressor. I also had to re-position the venturi in the pond bottom twice in this same time period after it had fallen over.

Without going into a lot of detail about specific test results, let me summarize the main revelations of operating this venturi system in my pond.

1. In September, the dissolved oxygen in the pond went from fairly well mixed from top to bottom, with the aerator running, to more pronounced stratification of dissolved oxygen (higher at surface, lower at bottom), as the aerator was off for longer periods of time.

2. During these tests, water transparency may improve modestly after the aerator was shut off, although this was not always the case.

3. In September, with the aerator off, the dissolved oxygen was well stratified (higher at the surface, lower at bottom) and then, with the aerator back on for 24 hours, the dissolved oxygen became very nearly equal from surface to bottom. I offer below one typical comparison of what this looked like:

Aerator off for long period   *Aerator back on for one day*
D.O. at 1 ft. = 11.0 mg/L   D.O. at 1 ft. = 7.6 mg/L
D.O. at 7 ft. = 0.8 mg/L   D.O. at 7 ft. = 7.2 mg/L

One can surmise from the results above, that total dissolved oxygen may not have increased so much as its distribution became equalized vertically. Indeed, this same phenomenon was also true when testing the dissolved oxygen with the aerator on and off, at other times of the year. However, the contrast of dissolved oxygen from surface to bottom with the aerator off, is considerably greater in warm weather than when it's cold.

Pronounced contrast of water temperature in the pond of surface water, compared to deep water, does not usually begin until late June. The greatest contrast in water temperatures I measured, occurred once in June, when the surface was 76°F and the bottom 55°F (nine feet deep). When this contrast occurs, a contrast in dissolved oxygen usually takes place at the same time. This is partly due to the resistance offered to mixing by the two layers of differing water temperatures and density. When the dissolved oxygen does not mix, distinctive strata develops. The action of the aerator/circulator tends to break down these strata. If anyone tells you that shallow ponds will not stratify thermally, tell them to come see me.

In the fall, around the beginning of October, cooling surface temperatures begin to cause the pond layers to mix again. Even if one did not operate an aerator, this mixing would occur naturally, and the mixing lasts pretty much until the next June (see below).

September 27th
D.O. at 1 ft. = 11.8 mg/L
D.O. at 7 ft. = 8.5 mg/L

March 30th
D.O. at 1 ft. = 12.6 mg/L
D.O. at 7 ft. = 13.3 mg/L

(no artificial aeration occurring on either date)

Sometimes I would use the circulating action of the aerator to aid in the distribution of chemicals, when I would wish to treat aquatic plants or algae in the pond. It was a simple matter to pour the prescribed amount of chemical on top of the peak of bubbling at the surface and let the circulation do the rest. This worked moderately well as a convenience, however, if I wished to get optimum coverage with chemicals, I found it was preferable to spray over all the area of intended plant control.

Along with the following die-off of the aquatic plants would invariably come lower dissolved oxygen in the water. This was due to the demand for oxygen created by the decomposition of the plants. Another event which would cause low dissolved oxygen, was a substantial runoff of sediment into the pond following intensive rainfall. The suspension of large amounts of sediment in the water would cause both high turbidity, and accompanying high demand upon the existing oxygen.

During the years in which I operated this venturi system, we did not experience a suffocation of fish, even though dissolved oxygen got quite low on a few occasions. The pond also did not experience a winterkill of fish during these 4-1/2 years. I noticed neither a reduction in algae, nor rooted aquatic plants, brought about by the long-term operation of this aerator system, which I removed in 1983.

When I would start the aerator in the winter under the ice cover, the resulting circulation would break through the ice. How soon it would break through would depend upon the thickness of the ice. It may take only fifteen minutes, or it might require half a day to create open water above the venturi. The size of the open hole also depended upon air temperature. In milder winter temperatures, the hole may be 75 feet wide (Figure 16), while in cold temperatures, it may only be ten feet in diameter. When the aerator was running for long periods of time in the ice, the ice may be several inches thick up close to the open hole, sufficient for the deer and other animals to sometimes walk out on the ice to drink out of the open water.

The operation of a second type of aerator system could not prevent suffocation of fish in June of 1993, after nearly five inches of rain fell in 24 hours. This artificial aerator also could not prevent fish suffocation in June of 1990, when I treated aquatic plants chemically, and a day later a very heavy rainfall occurred.

This second type of aeration system I installed is a horizontal, perforated plastic, 1/2 inch tubing which is 100 feet in length, and lies on the bottom of the pond in the deep area. Using a smaller compressor of 1/3 h.p., 115 volts and 9.0 amps, air is forced into this tubing and it then escapes up to the surface as small bubbles through tiny slots, spaced out every three inches along the tubing's entire length (Figure 17). The tubing stays on the bottom because it is weighted along its length with a lead keel. I replaced the original venturi system with this new one in May of 1983. With the help of one of my sons, I found it easy to install the tubing off a large, wooden roller and it worked properly right away. The principle of the long line of small bubbles of air is purported to be that they will more easily be assimilated by the water. The rising bubbles also cause circulation, like the venturi unit.

When I calculated the electrical cost of running this smaller compressor, I came up with 66¢/day, or $20.00/month. I'm sure this is not exact, but it's a close approximation. This also jibes pretty well with the differences in my electric bill when the aerator is running vs. when it is off for an entire month. The initial cost of this second system, compressor and all, was $600.00 in 1983.

Over a period of ten years, I also experimented with this second aeration system, testing water quality with it in operation for varying lengths of time, and also when it was not operating for various lengths of time. In all, I conducted 176 days of testing in various modes. Seasonally, 23% of the tests were in springtime; 47% summer: 15%: fall and 15% winter. Periods of time when the aerator had been in an operating mode varied from four hours to seven weeks, and when it had been shut off for periods of time, varying from fifteen hours to seven months.

The kinds of water quality tests centered mainly on the distribution of dissolved oxygen and temperature from the surface to the bottom: however other, additional kinds of water tests were sometimes taken. In the past three years I also occasionally conducted simultaneous tests in different parts of the pond for comparison. My usual test location was over the deepest water, about forty feet away from the air line, but I also tested in shallow, weedy areas and at the location where the water enters the pond, and where it goes out over the spillway.

A typical example of the effect of this aerator system in the summer, when it had *not* been operating for a week, vs. when it was turned on for 24 hours, is listed below:

	July 5th (off 6 days)		July 6th (on 24 hours)	
Depth (ft.)	Diss. oxygen (mg/L)	Temp. (°F)	Diss. oxygen (mg/L)	Temp. (°F)
1	10.9	75	7.8	76.5
2	9.2	73.5	7.4	75.5
3	6.7	72	7.4	75
4	4.0	71	7.4	74.5
5	2.0	69.5	7.3	74.5
6	1.2	68.5	7.3	74
6½	1.1	67.5	5.7	73.5

Notice the considerable contrast in both dissolved oxygen and temperature from top to bottom with the aerator off, compared to the more equal distribution of both, once it had been operating for 24 hours. The total dissolved oxygen in the water was also somewhat greater with the aerator operating. This effect was also noticeable on other occasions and suggests that this fine "bubble line" may be more capable of actually introducing dissolved oxygen to the water than the previous venturi system. It must be acknowledged that on a few instances in the summer, the pond stratified despite the operation of this aeration system.

I conducted seventeen water tests in the summer, comparing dissolved oxygen levels at similar depths with the aerator on and off, both close to the aerator, and in a remote part of the pond, a shallow area with aquatic plants. My purpose was to test if there was a substantial difference in oxygen levels between these separate locations. There seemed to be more of a contrast in these locations when the aerator was off, rather than when it was on. When the aerator was operating, there seemed to be little difference between these separate test areas, suggesting that it is affecting areas at least ninety feet removed from the air line.

In comparing the relative transparency of the water (May to October) with the aerator operating vs. when it had been off for a period of time, I can reach no conclusion. Sometimes the water was clearer with the aerator operating, but just as often it was not. Fifty percent of the time it seemed to make no significant difference one way or the other. I did notice that when plankton algae was concentrated near the surface, the clearer, deep water—devoid of algae—when it was circulated upward, made clear water just above the aerator, but not elsewhere. My advice would be: Don't buy an aerator with the main purpose of making your water clearer.

The effect of operating the aerator on the pH of the pond water is not consistent. Ordinarily, during warm weather, the pH of the surface water is somewhat higher (more alkaline) than that of deep water. This is likely a function of the metabolic activity of greater algae concentrations near the surface. Most of the time, when the aerator is operated and accompanied by water circulation, the pH of the surface water is lowered (e.g. pH 8.3 to pH 7.6). On rare occasions, particularly in the springtime, the opposite may occur, i.e. the surface pH becomes higher with aeration. More consistently, when the aerator is operating, the pH, like the dissolved oxygen, becomes more equalized from top to bottom. This could prove to be an asset when, for example, treating algae at the surface with copper compounds. Lower pH enhances the toxicity of the copper to the algae and may result in better control. However, under this scenario, the copper will also become more toxic to fish and other aquatic animals.

Another major attribute of providing aeration to a pond or lake, is that of creating a higher dissolved oxygen environment in the deep water that is in contact with the bottom mud, thereby limiting the emergence of phosphorus from the mud. This phosphorus would otherwise be circulated into the upper water and there may stimulate excessive growth of algae and other aquatic plants. In the midwest area where our pond is located, phosphorus is often considered the principal element stimulating the extent of growth of algae, thereby in limiting its presence, one may also (ostensibly) limit algae in locations where it may be too abundant.

While I did not specifically look at phosphorus levels during most of my "on" and "off" aerator experiments, I do have a few coincidental tests for total phosphorus in both aeration modes.

The limited evidence I have suggests that I find lower total phosphorus in the pond water with the aerator operating than when it is off. Ammonia nitrogen also seems to follow this trend, however, nitrate nitrogen does not. Because I have observed abundant algae in my pond, both with the aerator operating and with it off, I would hesitate to suggest that operating an aeration system is the solution to algae problems, I repeat, that there is *some* evidence that the phosphorus level in the water may be reduced with aeration.

When this "bubble line" aerator was turned on under an ice cover, it took much longer to break through the ice on top of it than did the venturi. This is no doubt due to the fact that the area of bubbles and circulation was much more concentrated in the venturi system than with the thin, long line of bubbles. To take a half inch of ice off the surface above a venturi would require less than an hour, whereas with the bubble line system, it may take several hours. However, once the water was open above either air system, it would not ice over again until the aerator was shut off.

The second, smaller compressor that I used (1/3 h.p.), I could hear on a quiet day from a distance of about 200 feet. The larger compressor could be heard from twice that distance. Mounting and shielding of the compressor also makes a difference. Five foot by four foot composition boards mounted on both sides of my compressors helped to mute the sound of the operating motor. I have done this both for creating more tranquility around the pond, but also to avoid disturbing animals in the wooded area where both the pond and compressor are located.

One management measure which either aeration system would provide by virtue of its removing an area of ice above it, is to allow greater sunlight penetration into the water. This is true both in the open water area and in the iced area of the pond immediately adjacent. In this manner, the plankton algae present in the water was able to produce dissolved oxygen at a much more rapid rate than when the ice and snow cover was present. I found by the simple measure of running the aerator for a day or two, I could provide this clear area of perhaps 1/5 surface acre, and profoundly influence the dissolved oxygen in the whole pond. Presently, I wait until snow cover gets more than two inches thick and lasts more than ten days, I turn on the aerator for a day or so and then turn it off. Even when it freezes over again this gives me the necessary clear ice until the next significant snow comes. This might not work with a single aerator in a pond much larger than mine.

Some of the snafus which have occurred in operating the compressor and air line include:

1. The compressor brushes get stuck when the unit filled up with ants;

2. My father backed into the compressor with a tractor and knocked it off its post;

3. The compressor bearings wore out;

4. My son-in-law, Ted, accidentally shot holes in the airline when target practicing with a rifle along the dam;

5. Ants also filled up the electrical outlet into which the compressor is plugged and thereby shut it off;

6. Mice and/or hornets have made nests within the compressor housing, perhaps attracted by the warmth of the operating unit during cool weather.

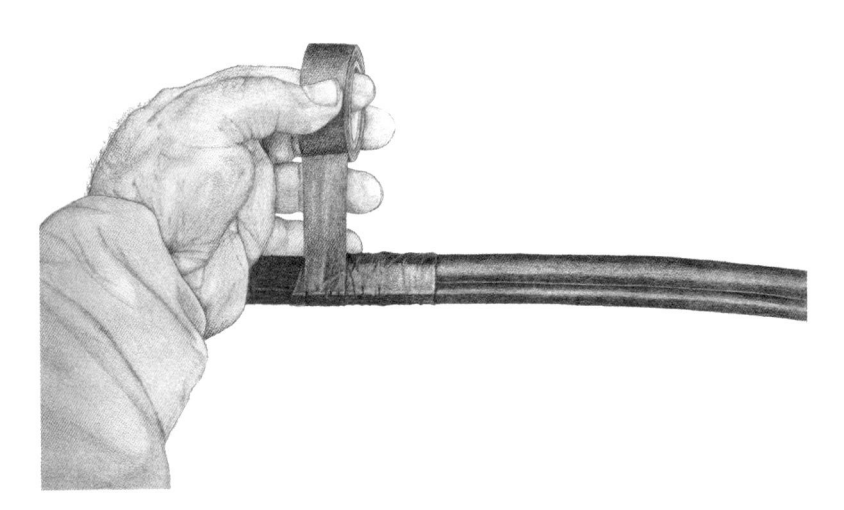

Figure 18. Taping hole in air line.

Also among the major snafus is the fact that muskrats consider the plastic air line under the water an irresistible delicacy, so they tend to chew on it a lot. I repair the holes with electrician's tape (Figure 18) at least twice a year and have had to install an entirely new line this year. Ponds where the air line is located in deeper water than mine, i.e. over ten feet deep, do not seem to have as much trouble with muskrat nibbling.

The first thing I do when I find the compressor is not fully working, is to check to see if the main switch is on. I then check to see if it is plugged into the socket, and finally, if the compressor is humming, but not fully operating, I shake the whole compressor vigorously. Starting it by the latter action has often saved me the embarrassment of sending the unit in for repair, but it also angered a hornets' nest once, to my consternation.

If the compressor is located a long way from your regular line source of electricity, it may also fail from causes like: (1.) When line power fluctuates, or gets low, the compressor shuts itself off, and (2.) If the line electric power blinks off for a fraction of a second, the compressor shuts itself off and doesn't restart. In both instances, it acts like a blown fuse, but that is not the case. In either instance the compressor may not start itself again when the power comes back up to normal. The shorter your extension line to the aerator compressor, the less trouble you will have. Unfortunately, my compressor is at least 300 feet away from my line power in the barn.

From the tracks that are apparent in the snow, I can tell that animals, like deer, will come down to drink out of the open water in the ice that the aerator creates. We have yet to see an animal that was drowned under these circumstances even though it would seem possible. Our golden retriever has fallen through the ice next to the aerator's hole at least once, but was able to get out again, presenting herself at the back door with a wet coat in midwinter.

Alkalinity and pH

The term "alkalinity" is a reference to the quantity of compounds in water which shift the pH to the alkaline side of neutral.

The alkalinity or acidity of waters is often measured in units known as "pH", on a scale of 1 to 14. A pH of over 7.0 is called "alkaline"; and below 7.0 is "acid"; the further away from 7.0, the more acid or alkaline is the water. Most lakes I have tested in the midwest have a pH of between 7.0 and 9.0, meaning most bodies of water here tend to be alkaline, or high in dissolved solids.

When the pond first filled with water, after construction, the pH measured between 7.1 and 7.7 for a year and a half. As soon as aquatic plant growth began to appear, the pH quickly elevated to 8.1 to 9.0 most of the warm weather months. Growth and photosynthesis of aquatic plants also tends to raise the pH (alkalinity) of the water, while death or absence of aquatic plants tends to lower the pH toward neutral. At no time has the pond water tested on the acid side, i.e. below a pH of 7.0.

Because aquatic plant and algae growth is most active during the warm months (May October), the pH of the pond water is also higher at that time. Over the years, the surface pH has averaged 7.7 in the winter months and 8.1 the rest of the year. One important factor in the lower pH observed in the winter is the fact that snow and snow melt is "soft water" and is very low in dissolved minerals. It has measured from pH 6.7 to 7.0 in the watershed of the pond. When I would kill aquatic plants with chemicals, or they would die from some other cause, the pH would typically become lower during the period of plant decomposition. Over 100 tests of pH covering every month of the year have contributed to these conclusions.

Another consistent phenomenon was that when I test surface water and deep water at the same time, the top water would almost always have a higher pH, sometimes considerably higher. When the aerator system was operating, the mixing of the water column tended to make the surface and deep water more similar in pH, with the pH becoming an average of both waters. Because most chemical treatment of aquatic plants occurs at or near the surface, and because most chemicals are more toxic in waters of lower pH, this would imply that toxicity of chemicals to both the plants and animals is greater when the aerator is operating and mixing the water.

I would have speculated that the pH of the water was lower late at night than it would be midday, because of the more limited photosynthesis by plants at night; however the data I have collected so far, comparing night/day pH, does not support this theory.

Besides the routinely alkaline pH I get in water tests for the pond, I have conducted other chemical tests that confirm the alkalinity of the water in regard to the kinds of compounds which shift the pH one way or the other. Tests of the pond water for total alkalinity were 126 mg/L one year after the pond first filled, and 210 mg/L a year later. After another fifteen years (1982), total alkalinity measured 540 mg/L. Aside from the activity of living aquatic plants, water pH or alkalinity is also influenced by both the compounds in soils in the watershed and the soil in the bottom of the pond itself. Coal strip mine lakes 70 miles south of our farm, routinely have water with lower pH, some so acid that fish cannot live in them. Waters with pH consistently below 6.0 and water with pH above 9.5 can also be unsatisfactory for most aquatic life.

Waters that tend to be more alkaline, like our pond, usually require higher dosages of chemicals to bring about certain management measures. One example would be the need for using more copper sulfate to kill algae. As stated before, one may view this as a disadvantage; however on the other hand, more alkaline water also tends to lower, or "buffer" the effects of certain chemical toxicants, like acid rain, so aquatic life is better protected. The exception to this rule is ammonia nitrogen, which actually becomes *more* toxic to aquatic life with higher alkalinity.

The maximum range I have found within our pond is pH 7.0 to 9.2, with an average pH of 8.0. This would be characterized as "moderately alkaline" water and that most typical to this midwest part of the country.

Phosphorus

People commonly use phosphorus as a part of the fertilizer they apply to stimulate growth of their lawn or garden. In most lakes and ponds in the midwest phosphorus is the element, or nutrient, which frequently limits the amount of algae present. The more phosphorus (P) there is, the more algae. Because algae often reaches nuisance proportions in richer lakes and ponds, interest in measuring and controlling phosphorus may assume importance.

The other common, essential element in aquatic plant growth is nitrogen (N). Both N and P are the building blocks of plant growth. When I measure phosphorus in the pond, I also measure various forms of nitrogen. Nitrogen is usually present in much higher amounts than phosphorus. If the ratio of nitrogen to phosphorus (N:P) is more than 16:1, it is felt that phosphorus is the limiting nutrient to aquatic plant growth. If the ratio is less than 5:1 (N:P), nitrogen is limiting. Tests show that in my pond phosphorus has been limiting more than twice as often as nitrogen.

Aquatic biologists believe that if total phosphorus (all forms) in waters is present in concentrations of less than 0.03 mg/L, algae "problems" will not ordinarily develop. Initially, most phosphorus gets into a new pond from the soil. Although the ability of phosphorus to dissolve in water is relatively low, small amounts also come into a pond from both rainfall runoff water and from the flooded pond bottom. Later, after plant and animal life develop in the pond, phosphorus is deposited when the aquatic life dies and decomposes. Some comes also from leaves from nearby trees and from wastes of waterfowl and other animals which frequent the pond or its watershed. Where there is cultivated agricultural land in a watershed, phosphorus may also come from commercial fertilizers which are captured by the washing of soils into rainfall runoff. Unlike nitrogen, little phosphorus enters the pond from direct rainfall from the atmosphere.

Since 1975, I have taken twenty-nine tests for phosphorus in my pond. The total phosphorus concentrations in these tests has ranged from less than 0.01 mg/L to 0.94 mg/L. Seven of these tests have shown 0.03 mg/L or less total phosphorus. In the tests I have taken, more phosphorus seems to be present in the warm weather than when it is cold. This may be because the rate of organic decomposition is much slower in cold water than in warm, thus reducing the rate of phosphorus recycling.

I have also taken tests of the water coming into the pond from field tile, and the water leaving the pond over the spillway on the same day, for comparison. So far, water entering has been significantly lower in phosphorus than the water leaving, suggesting that ample phosphorus was already present within the pond basin by the time the pond was twelve years old. When testing pond water for phosphorus, one may find a tremendous variation in a period of time as short as two months.

In any event, the tests I have taken to date would suggest that our pond has enough phosphorus most of the time to stimulate a lot of rooted, submergent plant or algae growth ... and in fact, abundant growth is present. These tests on the pond also demonstrate by the wide variety of results, that it is not safe to judge the richness of a body of water in phosphorus just from three or four tests. Moreover, the phosphorus levels in the pond have consistently tested higher in deep water than at the surface, sometimes by an order of magnitude.

I say, "rooted, submergent aquatic plants *or* algae" advisedly, because in my experience, if the phosphorus becomes tied up in extensive rooted plant growth in the water, there is little available to cause a nuisance growth of algae. In other words, it seems to be a "one or the other" situation biologically. If I purposely kill back the rooted plants and let them decompose in the pond, the phosphorus released by these dying plants will almost invariably bring about an extensive growth of algae—usually the filamentous (mossy) kind. Once in awhile it may end up as the plankton (pea-soup) variety of algae, but rarely do they both occur at the same time.

Not a whole lot can be done to prevent phosphorus from getting into a pond. Some of the things I have done to slow down the process are:

1. Planting pine trees on the sloping hillside in the watershed above the pond which had been previously farmed to row crops. This almost eliminated soil erosion from this acreage in a matter of three or four years.

2. Building a grass waterway through the watershed leading to the pond. This cleaned up the runoff water considerably. However, I didn't get around to making the grass waterway until the pond was already ten years old.

3. Putting about 30% of the watershed cropland immediately above the pond into a ten year, set-aside, Conservation Reserve Program (CRP) with the U.S. Department of Agriculture. This land was seeded to ground-protecting grasses and has virtually eliminated any remaining soil erosion into the pond, other than from exceptionally heavy rainfalls.

4. When the dam was constructed, we got a successful seeding and germination of grasses and fescues, which protected the surface of the dam from erosion within the first full year. These grasses are still protecting it thirty years later.

All four of the conservation measures listed above have served to reduce the phosphorus entering the pond. Unfortunately, some of them should have initiated years earlier than what I did, thus averting some algae problems.

By the late '70's, we were having problems in the warmer months as early as late April with filamentous algae of nuisance proportions. By "nuisance", I not only mean that it was unsightly, but that it also interfered with fishing and swimming. Perhaps 40 to 50% of the pond's surface would be covered with a floating algae mat. Consequently, in 1984, I undertook another management measure to reduce the amount of phosphorus within the pond by "binding" it up with another chemical. This is discussed next in the following section entitled, "Phosphorus Management".

Phosphorus Management

By 1984, I had taken steps to control the amount of phosphorus entering the pond from the watershed through the several erosion control practices already discussed. In order to reduce the amount of phosphorus which had already accumulated within the pond, I initiated a more direct, in-pond treatment program in the summer of 1984.

This treatment consisted of applying a soluble compound of aluminum to the water, which removes phosphorus from the water and precipitates to the bottom in a bound, floculant form. This kind of treatment is most effective in lakes which are well-buffered in alkalinity, and where algae is a common problem. It is also effective in bodies of water which stratify thermally in warm weather and may lose dissolved oxygen in deeper water. Our pond qualifies for this kind of treatment, at least part of the time, because it is always fairly alkaline in warm weather; algae is frequently a problem, but more often filamentous algae rather than plankton algae, and the water sometimes becomes stratified in warm weather and occasionally loses its oxygen in deeper water. (The lack of oxygen in the water above the bottom mud greatly accelerates the release of phosphorus from that source.)

I chose to use the compound aluminum sulfate for this treatment. It is relatively inexpensive (about $25.00 per 100 lbs.) and I have had prior experience using it. The dosage rate for the pond was arrived at by conducting tests of pond water in one gallon bottles. I wanted to achieve a good, visible floculant with the aluminum sulfate, but I did not want the pond to become any more acidic than pH 6.2 as a result of the treatment. If the water were to become too acid, fish and other desirable aquatic life might be injured.

By measuring different dosages, I found I could achieve the visible, white floculant (Figure 19) and the pH level I wanted with one gram of aluminum sulfate per gallon. Calculating the total volume of water in the pond, it appeared I would need about 2,000 pounds for the treatment.

Twenty days prior to this treatment to inactivate phospho-

Figure 19. White floc. of alum.

Figure 20. D-phosA 11/3/94.

Figure 21. Pond winter scenes.

Figure 22. Ice skatng party.

Figure 22B. Measuring ice thickness.

Figure 23. Steve fell through ice.

Figure 24. Snow cleared off ice rink.

Figure 25. Winterkill of fish March '77.

Figure 27. Chara.

Figure 28. Secchi disc on filamentous aglae.

Figure 29. Cousin's family at pond in August '67.

Figure 29B. Hydrodictyn net algae.

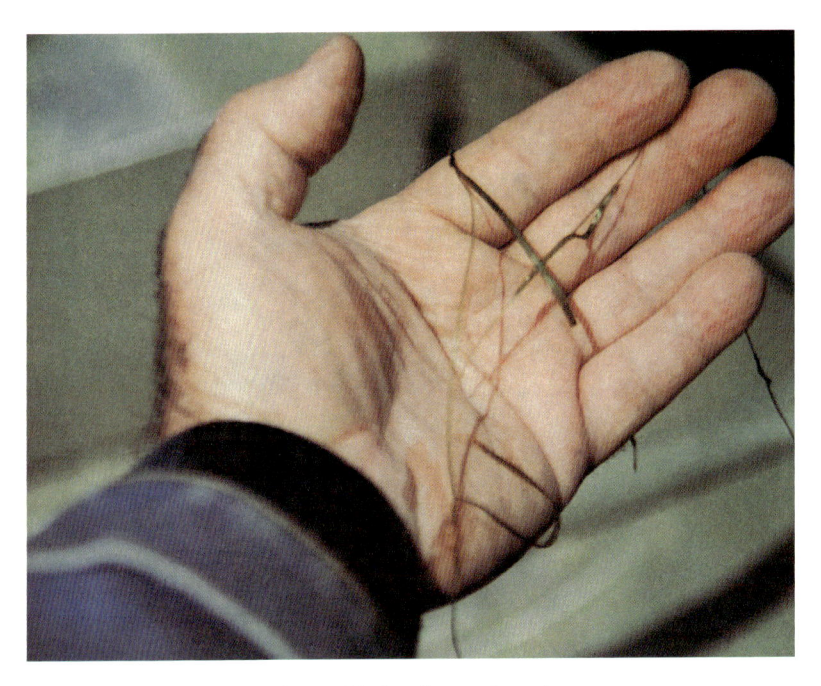

Figure 30. Leafy pondweed.

Figure 31. Illinois pondweed August '90.

Figure 32. Cattail leaves and seed heads.

Figure 33. Cattail tuber from pond July '92.

rus, I had applied a chemical to kill algae in the water. My aim was to allow much of the pre-existing algae to die, decompose, and release any phosphorus which was being held by the living plant tissues. Hopefully, this would make that organic phosphorus available as dissolved phosphorus in the water, and thereby susceptible to the inactivation process with the aluminum floculant.

On June 30, 1984, we made application of 1,000 pounds of aluminum sulfate. It was spread from a boat over the entire surface of the pond by mixing it as a slurry in a large, stock water tank, and then pumping it out as a spray. This took my son and me three hours to accomplish. I measured the pH and the transparency of the pond water before, during and after the application. I applied another 500 pounds of alum a few months later.

In the three hours of treatment, the water dropped from pH 8.0 (alkaline) to pH 6.8 (slightly acidic). Immediately before treatment, visibility in the water was 38 inches and twenty-four hours later it was 56 inches. A noticeable milky color was apparent in the water, and a white floculant could be seen settling to and covering the bottom. The floculant is actually a compound of aluminum. This condition was apparent for several days afterwards. All of these reactions—the lower pH, clearer water and white floculant, are expected results in such a treatment. Something not expected was the appearance during treatment of many small bluegills at the surface which seemed to be in some distress. The bluegills acted this way only for a few hours and then they behaved normally. I suspect that the quickly lowered pH caused this reaction. By the next morning, the alkalinity had gone back up to pH 7.4 and no fish nor any other aquatic animals had died.

Within two days a moderately strong, green plankton algae bloom was visible in the water, and within fifteen days the total phosphorus measured 0.32 mg/L in deep water, which was higher than it had been *prior* to the treatment. Water transparency had dropped to 18 inches because of the amount of green, plankton algae present. The fish, however, were behaving normally and were completing their spawning. By the end of July, small two-inch bass from that year's spawn were present in shallow water.

By September 7th, sixty-seven days after initial treatment, the total phosphorus concentration in the water had gone back down to less than 0.01 mg/L, and the water had begun clearing again. The first of November, water visibility at seven feet of depth was clear to the bottom, and the pH was back up to 8.5.

What then, are my conclusions about the value of this aluminum sulfate treatment in my pond? In fairness, I must say that I applied only about two-thirds as much chemical as I should have, partly due to an error I made in first calculating the total volume of the pond. The cost of the chemical used was less than $300.00, and the application was simple enough for the two of us to do from my 15-foot jon boat.

The transparency of the water for several years after treatment, averaged significantly clearer than it had for an equal period before treatment. Filamentous algae continued to be plentiful the next year following treatment, as did the submergent plants chara and leafy pondweed. I had hoped for a long-term reduction in algae so that I would not need to treat the pond chemically for control, but this did not happen. I found it was necessary to treat filamentous algae in 1985. I did not expect to get a reduction of rooted aquatic plants, and this proved to be correct. One year after treatment I could see no trace of the floculant on the bottom; however this was a drought year and low water levels exposed much of the pond bottom to drying.

This project may have been more successful had I used sufficient aluminum sulfate to begin with. It is possible even if I had, that I would not have achieved long-term control of filamentous algae. Despite this, the improved clarity of the water in itself almost made the project worthwhile. I'm not discouraged with this management technique and may try this method of treatment again, as I have had better success with it on ponds and lakes other than my own. The next time I'll spread the aluminum sulfate out on the ice cover in the winter. I experimented a little with this in 1991, and it seemed to work quite well. One can easily get good, even coverage of the chemical on the ice, and it appears to penetrate through the ice in a few days and to slowly enter the pond water as a solution. The pH of the pond is normally less alkaline in the winter, so I will need to conduct bottle tests of the water first, to be certain that I do not reduce the pH too much. I will also put proportionately more chemical over deep water than shallow areas. It will be revealing to see what happens the next year after application . . . the best laid plans of mice and men sometimes go astray, or "If at first you don't succeed . . ."

In 1994, I tried another method of phosphorus reduction. This involved the use of a commercial chemical preparation called DePhos-A (Figure 20), a product of Sweetwater, Division of TeeMark Corporation, Aitkin, Minnesota. It is buffered alum and very similar in its activity to the treatment I had completed in 1984, ten years earlier, in that it involved the use of the alum to precipitate phosphorus in the water. Chemically, it is 50% aluminum sulfate and 50% sodium bicarbonate. The instruction brochure suggests that this is a method of algae control on small bodies of water. The major differences from my former application of aluminum sulfate are that this treatment involved the use of a "buffered" alum and that it required much less product, about 90% less, compared to the amount of aluminum sulfate I had previously used. Forty pounds of this product were to be used for each acre-foot of water volume.

On the date of first treatment, November 3, 1994, it was a calm day and the pond level was quite low. I calculated there remained three acre-feet of water volume in the basin. Consequently, I applied three 40 pound pails of DePhos-A, which is about the consistency of table salt, by broadcasting it evenly over the surface of the water from my canoe. The chemical buffer was applied after each pail of alum. The total cost of this amount of product was about $230.00. It took me an hour and a half to make the application by myself.

Taking the alkalinity measurement of the surface water before and after the treatment showed a reduction from a pH of 8.5 to 8.0. Measurements of water transparency before and after showed that it had remained the same, 23 inches, and did not improve over the following week. No distressed fish were evident at any time.

Tests for total phosphorus in the water showed 0.16 mg/L, seven weeks *prior* to treatment and 0.06 mg/L ten days *after* treatment, indicating that although there was apparently a significant reduction in phosphorus, there still remained a sufficient amount to stimulate plant and algae growth. Indeed, there was substantial growth in the pond of both filamentous algae and water buttercup the following spring and summer.

Comparing the two methods, I believe I got more dramatic results using the large quantity of aluminum sulfate in 1984, than I did with the DePhos-A in 1994. It was certainly a whole lot easier using the lesser amount of commercial product . . . too bad the effect wasn't better. I must offer a word of caution here regarding relying too heavily on phosphorus tests. When comparing phosphorus tests from before and after treatments like this, you should best be using an average of *several* tests for at least two months before to five months after. Tests should also involve both surface water and deep water. On the other hand, one could always do things by the "seat of your pants" and forget about all the phosphorus tests. Just watch for what happens biologically to the body of water following any of these kinds of treatments. If you don't get noticeable reduction in algae over a long-term period following an application, then you didn't get the results you wanted.

Not one to give up, I gave DePhos-A another trial on October 27, 1996. Using much the same scenario as two years previously, I applied three 40 pound pails to the surface of the pond at a time when the water level was 2-1/2 feet below the spillway. This, as before, meant a considerable decrease in the pond's water volume and hence a decrease in chemical to be used. It will take me a while yet to evaluate this most recent application.

I.B.I. and T.S.I.
or
How Rich Can a Pond Get?

A wealthy man may define his richness by the diversity of investments in his portfolio. An aquatic biologist would define richness of a body of water in terms of the chemical quality of the water and by the number of species of plants and animals found both in and around that body of water. The equation is simple, the more species, the richer the environment. I know I have, or have had, at least seventeen species of larger, rooted aquatic plants in the pond. How many species of small plants and animals that may be classed as plankton, I do not know. I sent water samples to an algae expert once and he came up with a laundry list about a half a page long just of the algae species, only four or five species of which I recognized. The same applies to those kinds of wriggly aquatic animals, just barely visible. I know some of them, when magnified under a hand lens, but not many. It is comforting to me to have an awareness, at least, that there are a whole lot of different plants and critters that make the pond their home.

Of course, if one is a biologist, one has to put an acronym of some sort on everything to confuse the innocent public. In the instance of describing quality of the environment, we may use a kind of index method to relate that particular environment, like a pond or stream, to others in comparing different levels of quality. This we call *I*ndex of *B*iological *I*ntegrity (IBI). In a pond like ours, fish species are often subject to the stocking whims of the respective owner, but over other more mobile species, such as flying insects, one has very little control. However, the quality of the water where they may chose to deposit their eggs and spend much of their life *does* have a great deal to do with their survival. Kind of like the highway department may initiate speed limits on certain sections of roadway, the quality of the environment sets certain limits on the variety and abundance of the organisms which can survive there, hence the IBI.

In recent years, there has become another definition of quality of a body of water. I use "richness" in this instance to define how high a level of those nutrients, or elements, like phosphorus and nitrogen, might be present in the pond water at a certain time. These are the elements primarily responsible for too many aquatic plants, or too much algae of the wrong kind. In other words, what some may perceive as a problem growth of plants in a body of water.

Aquatic biologists may use a formula, other than the IBI species diversity, for measuring the richness of nutrients, so they use the concentration of total phosphorus in the water, the amount of green (chlorophyll) material present, and the extent of transparency of the water. The three measures are then compared on an arbitrary scale. The name used for this scale of measurement is called Carlson's *Trophic State Index*, or more simply TSI. The trophic state of a body of water may go all the way from very low in richness (TSI less than 40), to moderately rich (TSI 40 to 55), to very rich (TSI 60 to 80). This latter condition is called, "hypereutrophic". This is like running the gamut from a pristine, alpine lake to one of the sewage lagoons on the south side of Chicago.

As a body of water, like our pond, gets older, it usually gets richer, or more eutrophic. This is because elements like phosphorus tend to accumulate with increasing age of the pond's basin, such as increased inorganic and organic sediments deposited from incoming soil, and more dead plants building up on the pond's bottom. I have measured total phosphorus and water transparency in my pond hundreds of times since 1975. Following, I compare what the richness of the pond has averaged during two periods of time, 1975-1990 and 1991-1995. During the '75-'90 period, the TSI was 65 and from '91-'95, TSI was 63, i.e., hardly any difference. In any case our pond is shown to be pretty much on the "rich" side and hence very productive of aquatic plants, especially algae.

One could see this "rich" condition beginning to occur within seven years after the pond was constructed, with algae and higher aquatic plants becoming more abundant with each passing year. Why the pond hasn't shown even greater richness in the past four years, is a matter of interest. It may be that because the pond water level has been quite low in three of these four years and that the exposing of much of the bottom to sunlight and dehydration has allowed some nutrients to escape. It may also be that my attempt to tie up phosphorus with the use of aluminum sulfate in the summer of 1984, and again in February of 1991, met with some success. Since these treatments, the average water transparency of the pond has been slightly improved, which of itself could account for the richness index not rising. Also, the amount of cropland in the watershed was reduced about 50% in 1987, as a result of initiating a conservation practice. The phosphorus loading from the watershed into the pond is discussed in more detail in another section.

Finally, when one looks at the richness of a body of water, it is apparent that when it becomes too rich, whether it be too much in the way of nutrients, or the water area being taken over by too many aquatic plants, that species diversity is likely to diminish, and the water area becomes less useful and less life-giving. At that time it has gone, "over the hill" and efforts to bring it back will likely be both difficult and expensive.

A word of caution about using this method of establishing an "Index of Richness", or TSI: one must use a substantial number of measurements over a period of seasons and of successive years before placing much reliance on the results. I have conducted index measurements in the pond in the same year, that ran the gamut from TSI 40 (low in richness) to TSI 70 (high in richness). Weather, aquatic plant growth, season and time of day have much bearing upon one's calculated results. A minimum of ten TSI measurement over a period of five years, may begin to provide a suggestion of reliability. Just watching the variation of abundance and the persistence of algae increase over time may be just as good a clue as to what is happening in terms of increased enrichment in a body of water. For example, in the past three months, the pond has been virtually covered at the surface with filamentous algae. I didn't try to treat the algae chemically, however, I did run the aerator off an on during this period, and it made no perceptible difference in algae abundance.

This winter, I'll make another attempt at phosphorus reduction by applying alum to the surface of the ice (see Phosphorus Management section).

Nitrogen

Besides phosphorus, nitrogen is another element considered essential for aquatic plant and algae growth. Nitrogen can be present in several different forms in pond water. Nitrate nitrogen is the form most available to plants in water which has a lot of dissolved oxygen. High concentrations of nitrate nitrogen (above 1 mg/L) are usually found only near springs. Ammonia nitrogen may be present in water where organic decomposition or pollution is taking place and ammonia nitrogen is often used by certain species of noxious algae, although most plants seem to prefer nitrate nitrogen. Ammonia nitrogen can be toxic to fish when present above 2.5 mg/L; however, in my experience I have never seen fish killed in this manner in any body of water. Sometimes, in the presence of dissolved oxygen, ammonia nitrogen may convert to the nitrate form and hence become more available to plants.

The principal sources of nitrogen are from the atmosphere, in rain or snowfall, from bacterial action within the water, and input from surface or groundwater drainage into a pond. In farmland areas, nitrogen can come into a pond from water washing off fields which have recently received nitrate fertilizers or manure. A very possible source of nitrogen can also be from septic systems serving residences in the watershed. There are four residences served by septic systems within the watershed of my pond. These are in a subdivision developed about ten years after my pond was constructed.

Nitrogen, like phosphorus, tends to be present in greater quantity in deeper water during the summer. The buildup of forms of nitrogen under the ice may contribute to early spring algae abundance as has frequently happened in our pond. Tests of nitrogen either just before, or just after the ice goes out, have been uniformly high. Presumably, this is nitrogen that has not had the chance to escape to the atmosphere, because of the ice cover, and due to the greater solubility of this gas in colder water.

The relation of nitrogen to phosphorus has been discussed previously. In my pond, tests have shown a nitrogen:phosphorus ratio ranging from 3:1 to 75:1 and averaging 19:1. In the literature, "average" N:P ratio is said to be 7.5:1. Total nitrogen in a body of water is the sum of inorganic nitrogen and organic nitrogen The latter is sometimes referred to as "Kjeldahl" nitrogen.

Ammonia nitrogen has ranged from 0.01 mg/L to 0.40 mg/L and has averaged 0.19 mg/L. Nitrate nitrogen has ranged from 0.05 mg/L to 1.64 mg/L, and has averaged 0.60 mg/ L. I must mention here that most of the samples I have taken have been within one foot of the surface, which may tend in the summer to yield lower values in both phosphorus and ammonia nitrogen, than if I had taken them consistently in deeper water. Because nitrite nitrogen yields such low values in most bodies of water, I discontinued testing specifically for it after 1975. Tests which I took after 1980 showed totals of nitrate/nitrite nitrogen in combination. In most surface water, nitrite nitrogen is below 0.05 mg/L. I did not find any nitrite nitrogen concentration in my pond above 0.01 mg/L.

Operating the aerator system in the pond in warm weather appeared to reduce the amount of ammonia nitrogen, but not nitrate nitrogen. This would suggest that the noxious species of bluegreen algae may be lessened in a pond in which an aerator system is operating. Operating an aerator through the ice may also reduce nitrogen in the water; however, I cannot verify this from my experience with our own pond. In the winter of 1978-79, I did operate the aerator through the entire ice season, and yet the following May, the filamentous algae was as bad as ever.

It looks like plenty of nitrogen is present, in one form or other, in the pond, no matter what management measures I undertake. Because nitrogen is readily available from the atmosphere at most times, it is very difficult to try to control the amount which might be present in a pond or lake. To add to this dilemma, bluegreen algaes may fix nitrogen within their cells, storing it for possible later release. This helps to explain why when one kills algae in a pond, very shortly there often follows another algae abundance—perhaps not the same species, but one capable of replacement as soon as the nutrients become available. The dead or dying algae provides nitrogen and phosphorus for subsequent algae. This same scenario is also reenacted when other aquatic plants are either killed or die naturally.

Chapter 4

Seasonal Things Happening to Pond

Winter Conditions

Snow lay on the winter wheat
like comforting lamb's wool.
Field mice make their tunnels
safe from the circling redtail hawk.

Snow lies on the ice of the pond
as a downy blanket pulled over a window,
which causes continued darkness
to the water creatures below.

Or snow gathers in rivulets
like the windblown desert sands,
herringbone designs
decorating the suit of Mother Earth.

Corn stubbles jut out as sentinels
through their field of white,
skeletons which portend the melting snow
will nurture new life on Her breast.

Author

(Figure 21)

    I get a kick out of seeing the vast changes that occur at the pond with each of the four seasons. Right now, the leaves from the oak trees have mostly fallen and float for days at the pond's surface, soon to soak to the bottom and become a part of the growing organic sediment.

    The three months of winter in our northern U.S.A., also bring about unique conditions for ponds and lakes. They become like capsules, enclosed on the surface with ice and not communicating freely with the atmosphere as they do the rest of the year. Captured gases and the restriction of sunlight by ice and snow cover bring about biological and chemical qualities in the water that can be far different from the open-water months. It is difficult for one to appreciate that only a degree or two of temperature change can cause such a vast physical change in a body of water.

One can wander freely across the frozen pond surface and imagine that this is monotony, and nothing is going on beneath his feet. Actually, most of the pond life is still there, awake or sleeping below the ice cover. Indeed, all aquatic *and* terrestrial life on our earthly ball would not exist except for the simple principle that ice floats.

Ice Cover

How long ice covers a body of water in the wintertime, how thick it gets, and what its quality is, has considerable influence not only upon how safe the ice may be for human traffic, but also what kind of biological activity is going on under the ice. Over the thirty-odd years of the pond, I have tried to keep an accurate record of when the ice first stays on the surface each fall or winter and when it leaves the pond the following spring. As one might imagine, this is not always easy to determine.

Before heavy ice cover comes, there are usually several preceding days when a skim ice may be on the pond, especially in the morning. Skim ice has appeared on the pond as early as November 1st and as late as December 12th. The average date of skim ice first appearance has been November 21st, over the past 26 years. Skim ice indicates not only that the surface water temperatures are getting down to 32°F, but also it signals in many waters, the beginning of migration of waterfowl to more southerly climes, and the hibernation of amphibious animals.

The heavier ice cover may also come on and go off several times before a more permanent ice cover is formed, freezing and thawing like a petulant teenage girl. Early last winter, the ice cover has already been on and off the pond four times before Christmas. On rare occasions, the ice cover may also melt off in mid-winter and come back on again for a substantial period of time. If you will forgive a little generalizing on my part, I offer the following facts concerning the ice:

1. Long term ice cover on our pond averages 105 days, or 29% of the year;
2. Average "ice-on" date for complete ice cover of some permanence is December 4th;
3. Average "ice-off" date is March 19th;
4. The earliest "ice-on" coverage was November 14, 1976, and the latest "ice-on" was January 3, 1965;
5. The earliest "ice-off" was February 24, 1992, and the latest has been April 9, 1965.

The latitude of our farm (42°N) is about the same as Kalamazoo, Michigan; Souix City, Iowa; and Rockford, Illinois (Figure L). One can appreciate that there is usually a long period of time each winter that a body of water in this general latitude

Figure L. Location of pond in northern Illinois.

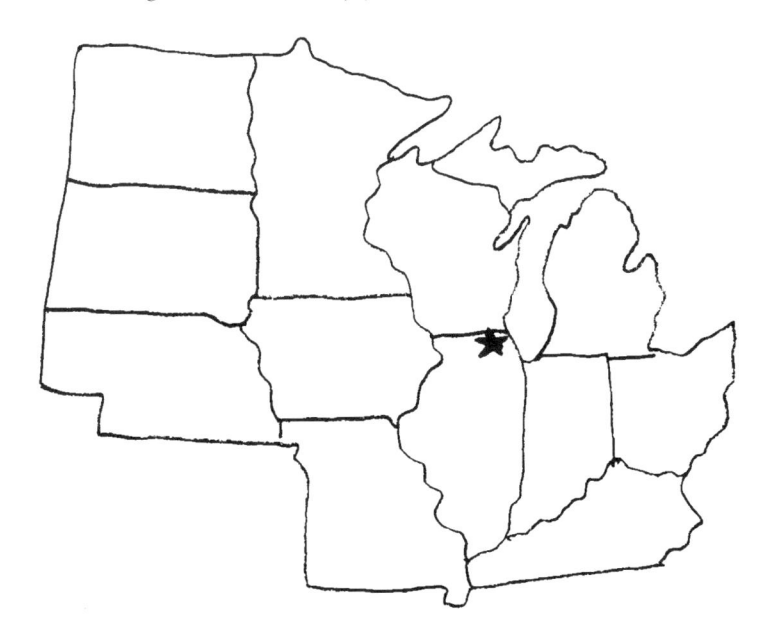

may be available for such winter sports as ice skating and ice fishing. Of course, lousy quality of ice (soft, ridged), or excessive snow cover may preclude enjoying either one of these sports. Indeed, these are the kinds of outdoor activities which may not be enjoyed by everyone to begin with, if one clings to the indoors and the TV when the thermometer gets below 30°F. I must say though, when our children were under sixteen years of age, they would frequently have ice skating parties on the pond with their friends (Figure 22). The two boys, Kevin and Pete, were likely to get up hockey games each weekend, with from five to ten other kids, all of whom may still have scar tissue to prove it . . . including the old man!

Fishing through the ice has always been popular on our pond and seems to appeal more to the "older generation" than to the youth. My observation about catching fish through the ice is that the fishing is usually better than it is during warm weather and open water. A little tip about keeping the surface of the ice smooth, like for ice skating, if you are drilling holes through it for some purpose: When you get finished with the use of the hole, just shove all your ice chips back into it. In that way the hole will freeze over again with no humps around it.

On certain days, I have made a point of measuring the thickness of the ice (Figure 22 B) at several widespread locations to see if it is uniform. Guess what? It is *not* uniform! For example, on February 23, 1991, ice at six different locations varied from 6-7/8" to 11-1/2". Quality of the ice also varies from week to week. Three inches of hard, clear ice is safer to walk on than eight inches of soft, honeycombed ice. A scary example of this occurred when a friend who was going to ice fish, fell through the ice (Figure 23) on January 30th. The ice was five inches thick, but was punky due to recent warm weather. Fortunately, he got himself out alright with nothing worse than a soaking (he was over deep water). The same thing happened to another ice fisherman on March 19th, but this was shortly before the ice melted entirely off the pond. The ice sagged when he walked on it, so it wasn't unexpected.

I must tell you a story along these lines, which is amusing

as I look back on it, but was not very funny to us when it happened. The two boys wanted to go down to the pond a few days after ice had formed. Kevin was ten and Peter was six years old at the time. I cautioned Kevin not to venture out onto the ice without testing it first by the shore. They came back shortly later to report the ice was, "O.K. to walk on". The next day I went to the pond and saw, to my bewilderment, a large rock sitting on the ice in the middle of the pond. When I questioned Peter about this he said, "Kevin told me to test the ice first, so he gave me the rock to take it out and drop it". Why parents get grey! I would not recommend this to anyone, but when I feel I must go out on ice which I think may be weak, I put on a pair of skis to distribute my weight more safely.

There has been two inches of ice cover as early as November 23rd, and ice has become as thick as 24 inches (March 8, 1978). There probably is no such thing as "average" ice thickness for certain winter dates, but I'm going to list below what I have found on a bi-weekly basis over the past 29 years:

Dates	*Ice thickness* (inches)	
	Min.	Max.
Nov. 14 - Nov. 30	0	2
Dec. 1 - Dec. 15	0	6
Dec. 16 - Dec. 31	0	8
Jan. 1 - Jan. 15	2	12
Jan. 16 - Jan. 31	4	16
Feb. 1 - Feb. 15	5	13
Feb. 16 - Feb. 29	0	15
March 1 - March 15	0	24
March 16 - March 31	0	13

The "average" ice thickness does not mean much insofar as how safe the ice may be to walk on. We have been able to walk on 2 inches of good ice in November and would not dare to venture out on eight inches of punky ice in mid-January. The first ice to form is usually clear, but later on, after snow has accumulated, thawed and refrozen on the surface, the top ice may become opaque. It is not unusual when one drills a hole through the ice, to see the upper half of the ice being opaque and the lower half quite clear.

After our experience of the kids dropping the rock on the ice, I make a point of going down to the pond every few days and drilling holes through the ice before we sanction either ice skating or ice fishing for anyone. One other of nature's coincidences occurs when the timing of the ice becoming unsafe late in the winter coincides closely with when the sap begins to flow in the maple trees.

Snow cover on the ice varies more than ice cover, both in thickness and how long it lasts. In the winter of 1979, the snow was so deep and persistent that we were hardly able to go down to the pond at all. It was often more than waist deep. Other winters, snow has varied from almost none to eight inches thick on the ice. In earlier winters, I would use my small tractor or my pickup truck to plow snow off the pond's surface, but one January I dropped the tractor (no pictures, please) through six inches of ice. Fortunately, I was over shallow water at the time and a helpful neighbor pulled me out from shore with his tractor and a cable. After that, I wait until there is eleven inches of good ice before I drive a vehicle onto it.

One object of doing snow removal was to create an ice skating rink for the kids (Figure 24), however I was hoping at the same time to remove sufficient snow cover to permit sunlight to penetrate the ice and stimulate photosynthesis by the aquatic plants and subsequent production of oxygen in the water. A thick snow cover on ice acts like placing a board over the grass on your lawn . . . no sunlight = no growth and soon the grass dies. Ice with no snow can permit considerable sunlight penetration into the water and keeps the aquatic plants perking.

In February of 1994, I plowed strips of snow from a large part of the pond. The snow cover had been present at various thicknesses for over a month and the dissolved oxygen content of the water was getting too low for either my comfort, or that of the fishes' (4.4 mg/L at three feet deep). For two days following my plowing of the snow, there was bright sunlight all day. The bright sun apparently penetrated the ice through the strips I had cleared and stimulated aquatic plant photosynthesis. The dissolved oxygen went up from 4.2 to 9.2 mg/L at three feet deep after 48 hours. By the way, there was twelve inches of good ice when I went out on it with my pickup truck and plow.

As long as there is water flowing into the pond from the tile which drains the watershed, there is a limited area of open area in the ice where this water enters on the southeast side. The size of this open water area depends upon the amount of flow and what the air temperature happens to be. It may be as small as nine, or as large as one hundred square feet. It does allow an area for oxygen to enter the water from the atmosphere. This is not "spring" water, but is ground water seepage, or surface runoff water.

This source of open water is also attractive to wildlife. I have frequently seen tracks of deer and raccoons there, but fox, pheasant, mink, muskrat, squirrel and rabbit tracks are also seen, along with the tracks of our own golden retriever and maybe a few stray dogs or a feral cat. Rarely do fish appear in this open area, except when the dissolved oxygen is low in the pond water. It is possible that this may help account for some partial fish survival when our pond has winterkilled.

Other Winter Conditions

Winter affords the amateur photographer a chance to get some unusual, seasonal shots, such as the first ice forming on the cattails, snow on limbs of trees framing the pond, along with animal tracks in the fresh snow. Winter also brings about different conditions to those creatures which live in the water. As one might suspect, activity of most plants and animals slows down a lot—plants and algae don't grow, instead diminish, or die—fish may bite timidly, or maybe not at all—water clears up more than usual. However, sometimes unusual things may appear. Pulses of aquatic animal plankton may make the water just under the ice look like it is teeming with little, wriggly things; a muskrat may poke its head up through a hole in the ice; muskrat houses made of cattails stick up through the ice, bluegills may also bite vigorously on an ice fisherman's bait; or the dissolved oxygen may get so high that the water appears to be effervescent like a soda water bottle.

Once I saw a pair of Canada geese standing on the ice in early March, like they were waiting impatiently for the pond to open up. I also saw three scaups one March 17th, paddling in the open water created in the ice by the aerator I was running. We have seen mud frozen into the ice as a result of a winter rainfall runoff, and have also seen filamentous algae frozen in the ice several times, and the same kind of algae popping up into newly drilled ice fishing holes along with numerous snail shells. Nature's little jewel box may be quiet, but it's not dead.

Winterkill

In the thirty-odd years of the pond's life, we have sometimes seen dead or dying fish appear shortly after the ice leaves the pond, either in March or April. On two successive "ice-outs", i.e. March of 1977 and March of 1978, substantial numbers of fish carcasses appeared at the surface as the ice cover diminished. This was a result of the phenomenon known by biologists as "winterkill".

Winterkilling is the suffocation of fish brought about by low, usually less than 3 mg/L, dissolved oxygen in the water under the ice. Water at 34°F is considered to be saturated with dissolved oxygen at 14.2 mg/L. Frequently, several factors in combination contribute to a low oxygen condition:

1. Dissolved oxygen is used up by organic decomposition in the water under the ice:
2. The production of oxygen by growing aquatic plants or algae is retarded, or ceases, due to a lack of sunlight penetration through ice. This is brought about by the opaqueness of the ice, the depth of snow cover on the surface of the ice, or both. Duration and thickness of both snow and

ice are equally important.

Five inches of clear ice permits nearly all the sunlight to penetrate into the water. Five inches of clear ice with one inch of complete snow cover, on the other hand, may allow only 10% sunlight penetration.

Nearly all the fish died in the winter of '76-'77. Permanent ice came on very early (November 14, 1976) and went off March 11, 1977. This was a total ice coverage of 117 days, compared to an average ice cover of 105 days. More importantly, the snow cover was also long in duration (over four weeks). At the same time, the water level of the pond was nearly four feet low all winter. I attempted to shovel strips of ice clear of snow several times; however the next windy day would find the snow blowing back over the cleared strips. My object, of course, was to allow sunlight to penetrate into the water more readily. Snow cover acts almost like a drawn window shade in blocking sunlight.

Drilling holes in the ice in February, disclosed small, dead bluegills floating up into the holes. When the snow cover finally melted off the ice in late February, I could see carcasses of fish frozen to the underside of the ice. The ice left the pond on March 11th, and large numbers of dead fish were drifting to the downwind shoreline (Figure 25). Although this was certainly a sad revelation for us, it did give me a unique opportunity to make an estimate of the fish population as it existed prior to the winterkill. I did this by measuring all the fish I could see and weighing a representative number. This was possible because the very cold water had kept the decomposition down to a slow rate, even though some of the fish had probably been dead for more than a month. After measuring the fish, I threw the larger ones over on the far side of the dam and put the smaller ones on my garden for fertilizer, as they say the Indians used to do.

My estimate of the fish population was as follows:

Largemouth bass

Length (inches)	Total number	Ave. weight (lbs.)	Total weight (lbs.)
under 5	10	0.03	0.30
5	10	0.06	0.60
6	35	0.09	3.15
7	15	0.16	2.40
8	3	0.25	0.75
9	7	0.37	2.59
10	24	0.53	12.72
11	26	0.71	18.46
12	28	0.95	24.70
13	18	1.21	21.78
14	15	1.50	22.50
15	7	1.87	13.09
16	2	2.36	4.72
17	1	2.93	2.93
18	2	3.53	7.06
19	3	4.38	13.14
			150.89

Bluegill

Length	Total number	Ave. weight	Total weight
2	3600	0.01	36.00
3	1800	0.02	36.00
4	600	0.04	24.00
5	400	0.09	36.00
6	320	0.16	51.20
7	130	0.26	33.80
over 8	40	0.44	17.60
			234.60

Northern pike

Length	Total number	Ave. weight	Total weight
20	2	1.68	3.36
22	3	2.30	6.90
			10.26

Fortunately, I found out that we had not lost 100% of the fish to winterkill. A few bass, a few bluegill and several northern pike survived, as I discovered in later testing. My estimate of the totals of each of the three species listed above is therefore conservative. In looking back, I believe I lost at least 85% of the bass and bluegills and perhaps 30% of the northern pike. Pike are known to tolerate lower levels of dissolved oxygen than most other fish species. Using a total weight of 396 pounds of fish, even this conservative estimate yields a standing crop of about 200 lbs/acre of fish for my pond.

The winterkill the next winter of 1977-'78, did not seem as extensive, however it must be acknowledged that the fish population had also had not much time to rebuild in a period of one year. I had stocked both largemouth bass, bluegills and some minnows in the spring of 1977. As early as March 28, I knew there was survival of northern pike and by May I had seen some bass survival and in July, I saw surviving bluegills. These fish were of a different size than those I had just restocked in the pond. This latter winter, the ice coverage was of even longer duration, i.e. 128 days, or more than three weeks longer than average ice coverage. The ice did not leave until April 2, 1978; however the pond level was full nearly all winter.

Further complicating the matter, the snow cover was especially long in duration and heavy, averaging four to eight inches. I tried keeping two spots of ice, 800 square feet each, clear of snow by shoveling. This again was to allow some sunlight to pass through the sixteen inches of ice and secondarily to provide ice skating areas for the kids. Ice fishing was very poor this winter. The first week in March, I drilled some holes through the ice, but could see not dead fish and the water had no odor, such as it had the prior March.

After the first of April, when the ice left, we could see a few carcasses of both bass and bluegills. Dead frogs were also numerous. Despite my efforts to keep about 15% of the ice clear of snow, the pond had winterkilled for the second successive time. Apparently the heavy snow cover for 126 continuous days overcame my good intentions. This also happened despite the fact that the pond was very nearly full of water all winter, whereas in the previous winter the water level was quite low.

In April, we began seeing the activity of live fish very soon. I caught eleven northern pike in a net on April 6th, but no other species. By mid-April, I had found a few live, yearling bluegills. I stocked nine 10 inch bass and on the same day, April 22, I found with a seine five yearling bass and a dozen yearling bluegills. By May, it was apparent that this winterkill had left a lot of survivors of all three species. largemouth bass, bluegills, and northern pike, and that it would not be necessary to do any further stocking of fish.

Can any generalizations be made out of these winterkill experiences? Maybe the following:

1. Winterkills of fish may be severe, but do not often kill all the fish;
2. Winterkills are aggravated by long-term ice and also snow cover:
3. Winterkills may occur whether water levels are low or normal;
4. Shoveling snow off a portion of the ice may, or may not prevent winterkill. A lot depends on subsequent weather conditions;
5. Some species of fish, like northern pike, may be less susceptible to winterkill than largemouth bass and bluegills;
6. Reproduction of surviving fish the next year after winterkill is quite good, as is growth;
7. Survival of young fish, hatched after a winterkill, can also be quite good;
8. Numbers 6 and 7, are likely a result of less competition and lower predation, reflecting the reduced density of the population;
9. Winterkill can give one a unique perspective on the number and sizes of fish a body of water can support. It might also make one wonder why he or she wasn't able to catch some of these many fish *before* the winterkill.

These experiences with winterkill of fish prompted me to install an aeration system in the pond as an attempt to avoid future winterkills. I did this in October of 1978 (see Chapter on Aeration). Since that time, I have not experienced further winterkills; however I have lost fish from low dissolved oxygen during the warm months.

A word of caution about lack of fish activity when the ice first goes out in the early part of the year. As I have stated elsewhere, one may see no evidence of fish activity when walking around the shoreline for many days after the ice clears off. Don't panic about the fish having died during the winter. If you see no dead fish carcasses floating around, the fish are probably still there, they just don't show much of themselves in the cold water and may be lurking in deep water, or under floating debris along the shore. Once the water temperature gets up to 50°F or so, you'll begin to see fish swimming around again, even though they might not bite yet on hook and line.

Chapter 5

Biological Things Happening to Pond

Bacteria

Bacteria in a body of water are essential to the maintenance of aquatic life. Besides breaking down organic substances to a simpler, more usable form which can be assimilated by aquatic plants and animals, bacteria can also be involved in the transmission of diseases in animals, all the way from fish to human beings. More often though, their function is beneficial. Were it not for bacteria, ponds and lakes would fill in much more rapidly with organic material and important food chains would be rendered useless. Because the function of bacteria and algae are so similar, they are often grouped together.

Coliform bacteria is often focused upon because of its negative implications. For many years, public health agencies have used the presence of various coliform bacteria in water, as a criteria for judging whether the water might be safe for humans to use for purposes like swimming or drinking. Because coliform bacteria are associated with the intestinal tract of warm-blooded animals, their presence in water suggests fecal pollution and because these bacteria are not long-lived in water, their presence also suggests recent contamination. Certain disease organisms may be associated with fecal coliform bacteria, so biologists may say that coliform bacteria found in sufficient numbers in swimming water portends the possibility of associated diseases. For water that comes into contact with the body, the "safe" level of fecal coliform bacteria is regarded as any number below 200 per 100 ml of water. Remember, these indicator bacteria don't come from fish, frogs or turtles, they come from waterfowl, cattle and from you and me.

A few homes are located in the corner of an oak woodland, which is within the watershed that drains to our pond. These homes utilize septic drain fields for domestic waste disposal.

Occasionally a septic field may not operate properly. In order to evaluate whether there might be septic escape from these homes which could impact on the water quality of our pond, especially during periods of heavy rainfall runoff, I have taken seventeen separate coliform bacteria tests of our pond water. The majority of these tests were made from 1989 to '95.

In only one instance in these tests was the fecal coliform bacteria count greater than 200 per 100 ml; this occurred on September 11, 1992. At this time the water level of the pond was two feet below the spillway, and numbers of ducks and herons had been using the pond daily. A test taken twenty days later for fecal coliforms revealed only 68 per 100 ml, which is satisfactory. Possibly the low water level, coupled with the presence of waterfowl had elevated the coliform bacteria count temporarily in the one instance.

Another phenomenon which elevates coliform bacteria numbers in ponds is heavy rainfall runoff. This tends to wash feces of animals from the watershed more rapidly into the body of water. Because of the rapid reproductive rate of bacteria, I doubt if it is unusual for any pond or lake in the midwest to have occasional fecal coliform bacteria counts which are high. Bacteria are capable of doubling their populations in a matter of hours. It is a high frequency of coliform bacteria counts, i.e. 20% of the time or more, that should be regarded with suspicion. In our pond, at no time have I felt it necessary to close it to swimming because of bacterial contamination.

The source of fecal pollution can sometimes be determined by taking the number of fecal coliform bacteria found in a given sample, and dividing it by the number of fecal streptococci bacteria (FC/FS) found in that same sample. A ratio of over 4.4/1 is considered to be a human source, while a ratio lower than 4/1 is non-human. On October 3, 1994, I took both samples to a lab and found a ratio of 0.7/1. This, according to water quality books, suggests that the probable source of fecal pollution is coming from waterfowl. Indeed, during the three weeks prior to these tests, our pond was being used almost daily by both bluewing teal and Canada geese.

Figure 26. Sterile bacteria bottle.

A word of caution—bacteria samples must be carefully taken in sterile containers (Figure 26) and promptly transported to a certified laboratory for analysis. It would be wise to contact the lab ahead of time for both instructions and for sterile collection containers. Some county health departments offer this service for the convenience of their residents. Also, I would not rely on just one sample for making a judgement about a pond. It would be best to take at least four or five separate samples during that part of the year when swimming might occur.

Regarding the beneficial aspects of bacteria in water, there have recently been sales promotions of commercially prepared bacteria cultures as a safe method of "cleaning up" lakes and ponds. To me, this is much as I would visualize using the bacteria formulations which are sold for "seeding" septic tanks and septic systems, thereby improving their efficiency. We have used such inoculations in our own rural septic system, but whether it has had any benefits, I have no way of knowing. The process *sounds* so good that I would like to try it in our pond, if I could only figure out some controls to test whether it's doing anything positive or negative in improving the decomposition of organic matter. The other question that concerns me is: "What's wrong with all the kinds of bacteria which we have naturally?" Mother Nature has been providing the environment with a jillion different species of bacteria to do these various jobs for much longer than mankind has been around.

Plants In and Around the Pond and Attempted Control Measures

What I want to talk about here is mainly those plants which have appeared within the perimeter of the water's edge, either aquatic or wetland plants. When the pond was constructed in 1964, all vegetation was scraped away from the pond basin and the area immediately adjacent by earthmoving equipment. Other than those grasses which we seeded on the dam, all the other subsequent plant growth appeared voluntarily.

First to appear in the newly pooled water of the pond were the algaes and they were present, no doubt, from day one. They will even appear in temporary mud puddles. Algae were not conspicuous, however, until the next year after the pond began to fill; by May or June, both chara (Figure 27), a submergent, complex algae, and filamentous algae became noticeable. Leafy pondweed, a rooted, submergent aquatic plant, also first appeared by June of 1965. By June of 1966, both chara and filamentous algae (Figure 28) had become sufficiently abundant in growth so that I thought I should attempt some chemical control, as the children were now using the pond for swimming (Figure 29).

Before I proceed further, let me qualify what I mean when I use the word "algae". I can readily identify only a few species of algae at hand, such as chara, *Euglena, Spirogyra, Cladophora* and *Hydrodictyn* (Figure 29B). Others would require a microscope for me to identify. As a consequence, most of my reference to algae from now on will be either "filamentous" (multicellular filaments, either floating or submerged), or "plankton" (usually one-celled and submerged). The algae are most important in the ecology of a pond, as they are the primary converters of inorganic nutrients to an organic form which can be utilized as food by higher life forms, such as small animals. They are sometimes difficult to distinguish from bacteria, except that algae usually have cells containing chlorophyll. Diatoms are also simple plants, however they are brownish in color, rather than green. There is a seasonal progression of algae and diatoms in most ponds like mine which proceeds as follows: Spring = diatoms and green, filamentous algae; Early Summer = green algae; Late Summer = bluegreen algae; and Fall/ Winter = diatoms again. Higher forms of aquatic plants, unlike algae, have true stems, leaves and roots.

In the course of thirty-odd years, at least 17 species or groups of larger aquatic plants have appeared within, on, or next to the pond. Most of these species have persisted over the years since their first appearance, despite my attempts to control them, either chemically, manually, or biologically. Only the bulrush has appeared for several years, and then seemingly disappeared. One species, *Nitella,* which looks a lot like chara, except that it doesn't have the crusty leaves and musky odor, showed up last year for the first time. Why this after thirty-plus years, I don't know—I've seen it in far fewer ponds and lakes than chara.

Many of the states, through their Departments of Natural Resources, make booklets available to the public concerning the identification of aquatic plants and possible methods of control. Illinois has a good one.

Probably the main stimulus to the expanding growth of submerged and emergent aquatic plants in our pond, has been the presence of shallow water. Over 70% of the pond's area is less than six feet deep, and most of this area is subject to submergent plant growth. Around the pond's perimeter in water less than three feet deep, plants such as cattails, reed canary grass, smartweed and arrowhead find suitable growing habitat. One small portion of the southern shoreline is under the shade of mature oak trees during the warm weather. This shaded area has very little in the way of aquatic plant growth. The moral to this story is if you wish to control rooted, submergent plants in a new pond, *first* plan to make most of the pond depth deeper than six feet, preferably nine or ten feet deep. In this manner you will limit the rooted plant growth simply by placing the pond bottom *below* the depth of sunlight penetration. This will save a person many headaches and heartaches attempting to control plants after the pond is built. The excessive shallow water area in my pond was my major boo-boo in designing it. Ducks and geese, frogs, turtles and toads may love a body of water full of aquatic plants, but most people do not share this joy.

Over the the pond's life, I have treated the aquatic plants 115 different times in the process of using 16 different kinds of chemicals (Figure C). Most commonly, I have treated the filamentous (mossy) algae. This is because it looks so bad when abundant on the surface, and also because it regrows so rapidly after it is killed. Mainly I have used copper sulfate, or a copper compound named Cutrine, in algae control. Occasionally, I have combined the copper compound with another chemical, Diquat, to enhance its toxicity to algae. I have also combined copper sulfate with citric acid, which prolongs its toxicity in alkaline waters. Rate of treatment with copper sulfate has varied all the way from 1-1/2 to 11 pounds per acre of water and has averaged six pounds per acre. When I mix in dry citric acid, I mix it 1:1 with the copper sulfate. I usually dissolve the mixture in water and then, using a pump from a boat, spray it over the surface of the pond or simply broadcast it with a dipper. The Cutrine is available in either liquid or granular form. I soon found out that the copper sulfate with citric acid was just as effective in killing algae as the commercial formulation and was much cheaper. I had varying degrees of success treating algae during the months of May through July, but even if I was successful in eliminating what I thought was an algae problem for a couple of weeks, it soon came back.

When I used a mixture of the chemical Ortho Diquat *(Reward)* with the copper solution, it was at a ratio of one pint to five pounds. This gave a much more thorough kill of the algae plus some of the other aquatic plants, but the algae still came back. An application of five pounds of Karmex plus five pounds of Aquazine (the granules mixed into a solution) also worked well on algae as a broadcast or spray, however, I don't believe Karmex is available anymore and also the label states, "Do not use in water".

Nowadays, if one wishes to use a commercial chemical for plant control, one must face the rigor of trying to figure out the best manner in which it should be mixed and applied. Since about 1980, the instructions on the chemical labels deal mainly with the precautions to be used and the manner of treatment for toxicity of the chemical to the skin, eyes or by ingestion. This may all be warranted, but the poor applicator must search diligently to find that meager sentence or two which describes the best method of application, if indeed he can find it at all.

A few years ago (May, 1994), I attempted to control filamentous algae with a combination of 5 pounds Karmex, mixed with 5 pounds. of Aquazine. I got surprisingly good control of the algae however water buttercup was coming in at the same time and this mixture also killed that species of plant. Because Karmex works by inhibiting photosynthesis, I not only lost oxygen production by any green, living plants, but I also brought about a severe reduction of dissolved oxygen due to the plant material decomposing in the pond. Although I ran my aerator, the dissolved oxygen dropped as low as 2 mg/L at the surface and less in deeper water. Fish began showing stress of suffocation five days later. Nothing in instruction labels tell you about this, but the Karmex label does state, "Do not use in water".

To kill species of plants such as leafy pondweed (Figure 30), I have used the chemical Ortho Diquat many times, usually at a rate of one-quarter to 1 gallon per surface acre. I have also used Ortho Diquat, now known as Reward, as a spray on cattails. Diquat causes the plants to turn brown within a few days and although it may completely kill leafy pondweed, the brown cattail leaves become green again from the newly growing parts under the water. I have tried Hydrathol 47 and potassium endothal also on submergent plants. I had trouble with low dissolved oxygen and fish dying when I used Hydrathol 47 in May of 1967. In 1977, I switched from potassium endothal to Aquathol K and had fair success with it, treating leafy pondweed.

Figure C. Herbicide chemicals as mentioned in text and data as found on containers.

Trade Name	Chemical Name	Amount of Active Ingredient	Manufacturer on Container
Aquathol K	dipotassium salt of endothall		AgChem Div. Pennwalt Corp.
Aquazine	2-chloro-4, 6 bis (ethylamino) s-triazine		Ciba-Geigy Corp.
Casoron	dichlobenil		
Copper sulfate	copper sulfate pentahydrate	99%	Phelps Dodge Refining Corp.
Cutrine-Plus	copper as elemental	9%	Applied Biochemists, Inc.
Ortho Diquat Now "Reward"	salt of 4,4' dipyridyl dibromide		Chevron Chemical Comp.
2,4,5-T	no container found		
2,4-D liquid	2,4-dichlorophenoxy acedic acid		Interag Corp.
Hydrothal 191	mono (N,N-dihethylalkyhamine) salt of Endothall		Ag-Chem Div. Pennwalt Corp.
Hydrathol 47	no container found		
Rodeo	isopropylamine salt of glyophosphate	53.8%	Monsanto
Sonar AS	Fluridone		SePR0 Corp.

For chara, the higher algae which looks like a pondweed, in addition to the copper compounds, I began using Karmex from 1982 to '87, at a rate of 1 lb/acre. I did not seem to have any greater success with this more expensive chemical than I did with the copper compounds, although as I stated previously, the Karmex *was* effective in killing filamentous algae. I also used 50 lbs/acre of Cassoron, which was ineffective.

For rooted submergent plants like leafy pondweed and water buttercup, I also used Hydrothal 191 liquid in three different years, but after causing a significant fish kill in June of 1990, I discontinued using it. The most recent chemical I have used is Sonar AS, a liquid. This chemical differs from the others in that it must be applied very early in the season (April), even before the plants become apparent. It also kills rather slowly and over a long period of time, perhaps taking two months to eliminate the plants. It has very little effect upon the various kinds of algae, but sometimes it will effect cattails, turning them white. I have had trouble with prolonged low dissolved oxygen after using Sonar in my pond for water buttercup, but have rarely had this problem in other lakes, using it on different species of rooted submergent plants.

In 1974, I used a blue dye, Aquashade, in the pond. It has been touted by some sales people as a means of controlling submergent aquatic plants by blocking off sunlight penetration into the water. In the period of a month (July), after keeping the water a deep, turquoise color through added treatment I could see no effect on any of the aquatic plants. Some of the blue color was still apparent eight months after application. If you want to make your water blue, go ahead with using the dye, but don't expect a significant effect upon the plants.

Some aquatic plants, such as water buttercup and filamentous algae, may be present as soon as the ice goes out, while others like leafy pondweed, Illinois pondweed (Figure 31) and cattails may not appear until mid-April or May. If ice and water conditions are clear in the late winter, a mat of green, filamentous algae, usually *Spirogyra,* may grow on the bottom in water less than six feet deep. Once the ice goes off, gases under this mat of algae may cause sections to rise and float to the surface in an unsightly manner. This is not a symptom of poor water quality, however.

In Figure PS, I have listed what I have found to be the seasonal appearance of certain plants. Cattails may not be fully emerged above the water surface until July and should not be treated chemically until then. Besides Diquat, I have sprayed cattails with Dowpon, 2,4-D, 2,4,5-T and Rodeo combined with a commercial carrier, or "sticker" to make the chemical adhere to cattail leaves (Figure 32). I have also used a liquid detergent in place of the "sticker" and it seems to work as well. Although I frequently kill the existing cattail growth with these sprays, they always come back strong the next year. Cattails have a large root system, or tuber (Figure 33), which stores much energy, and this root is apparently unaffected by the chemicals.

Figure 34. Fiber mesh sheeting on pond bottom.

Figure 35. Water buttercup in bloom.

Figure 36. Liverwort Riccia *from pond.*

Figure 36B. Bulrush in seed.

104

Figure 37. Purple loosestrife.

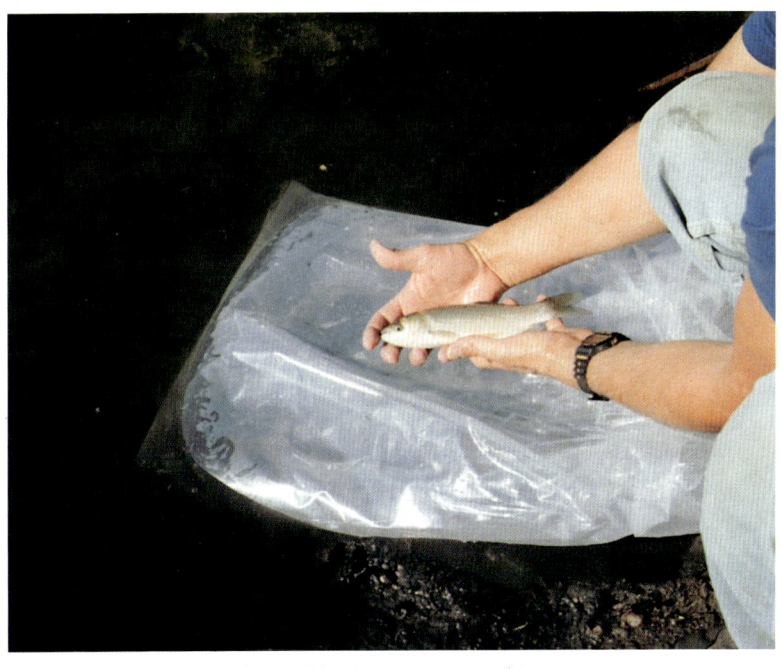

Figure 38. Grass carp stocking.

Figure 38B. Dead grass carp.

Figure 39. Adult dragonfly on canoe September '88.

Figure 39B. Dragonfly nymph.

Figure 40. Snail and clam.

Figure 41. Cornfield above pond.

Figure 42. Pesticide fish kill.

Figure 43. Picking up bass after fish kill.

Figure 44. Snapping turtle.

Figure 44B. Leopard frog.

Figure 45. Jake and bullfrog from pond.

Figure P5. *Seasonality of Aquatic Plants*

Filamentous algae
Some may be seen as early as March, frozen into the ice. The early filamentous algae is often seen growing on the pond bottom in April and May. By July and August may cover 30-75% of the pond's surface. Less abundant by mid-September.

Plankton algae
Not seen in abundance as much as filamentous algae, but can be present as early as late March. Also, may be present again later in the year, Sept.-Nov. If plankton algae is in bloom, there is usually very little filamentous algae.

Cattails
Begin sticking-out of the water by late April. Leaves may extend 18 inches out of the water by first week in May. Begin shedding seeds from heads by first of November.

Bullrushes
A foot high by first week in May. Goes to seed in October.

Chara
Begins to show up in late April and may become abundant by first of June. Persists through October and may be present under the ice. Does not blossom.

Water buttercup
Showing up by late April or first of May. Begins to bloom in mid-May. Loses white blossoms mid-July. Rank in May, June and July.

Leafy pondweed
Appears in late May, early June. May be abundant May - Oct. No conspicuous flowers.

Reed canary grass
This coarse grass appears in very shallow water & shore by early May, early June. May lay flat on the water, then later stand upright.

Figure PS. (continued)

Sago pondweed	Duckweed
May be abundant in September. No conspicuous flowers.	Shows up in early June. Floats at surface like a green mat due to its small size. Disappears in October.
Naiad	Smartweed
Abundant in July, persists into late Sept., early October.	Grows on exposed pond mud and shallow water in early summer. Goes to seed in October.

I have tried to control cattails by cutting them with a scythe, or if the water level is low enough, mowing them with a tractor mower. Once when the pond level had gotten quite low, I was also able to disc the cattails into the soil where it had been shallow water. Only once, in 1990, was I able to retard the next year's growth of cattails by chemical treatment. In 1990, I applied 2,4-D as a spray in the months of May, July and August. In 1991, few cattails came up, but in 1992, they were abundant again. The areas of cattail growth doubled from 1983 to 1995. The moral to this story appears to be to keep treating cattails several times during the growing season, and in that manner drain out much of the reserve energy in their large root (rhizome) system, weakening the plant enough so it cannot grow the next season. The mechanical control, using cutting, mowing and discing, did not seem to effect the next year's growth, so I've given up on those methods.

Another non-chemical approach to controlling rooted, submergent aquatic plants involves the use of plastic fiber-mesh sheeting which is placed on the pond bottom and secured there with weights or stakes. To evaluate this, I placed a piece of this sheeting 6' X 6' square on the bottom in three feet of water (Figure 34) and secured it with small steel posts. Unfortunately, the part of the bottom covered was relatively small, so it was difficult to see any difference in overall plant abundance after its placement. Also, even though the sheet *did* prevent rooted plant growth in that area, the filamentous algae grew on top of the sheeting so the bottom appeared green with plant growth. At least seven years after the sheeting placement, this area is still devoid of rooted plant growth, but still has algae off and on. Had I sheeted a much larger area, such as 50' X 100', it would have made a noticeable difference in rooted plant growth. The next time the pond level gets low and exposes much of the bottom, I will try to sheet a larger area.

An additional manual method of plant control tried was using a cutter bar, which is thrown out into the water and pulled back to shore with an attached rope. This bar, which costs about $90.00, is Y-shaped with the forked end of the "Y" being two cutter blades, at about a 60 degree angle to one another. The cutting edge is on the outer side of these blades; thus when pulled back to shore they are supposed to cut any plants encountered. I used this device a few times and decided it was mostly a waste of effort. If the plant growth was heavy, the weed bar would simply ride on top of them. If cattails were present near shore the blades could not be drawn through them. If filamentous algae was present at the surface it would bind onto the cutter blades and they would not cut. This "weed cutter" and a comparable rake is available from Aquatic Control of Seymour, Indiana.

What's wrong with having a few plants?

With all this discussion about the elimination of different kinds of aquatic plants, the reader may get the notion that plants must be detrimental to a pond. Although it is true that plants can be a nuisance to people if they are too abundant, more often, aquatic plants are beneficial to other life forms. The following list details some benefits of aquatic plants:

1. Plants provide good habitat for fish and aquatic insects, both as food and as hiding places for all species of small fish.

2. Rooted plants tend to make the water clearer and to hold down algae growth.
3. Many kinds of aquatic plants are highly sought after by waterfowl.
4. Aquatic plants tend to stabilize the bottom of a pond and its shoreline.
5. Plants are the primary converters of nutrients to a form useable by animals.
6. Emergent aquatic plants provide cover and nesting places for waterfowl and shore birds.
7. Aquatic plants contribute to water quality through production of dissolved oxygen.

In my professional life as a biologist, I have come to regard aquatic plants in a much more friendly light the older I get. This, I believe, is the result of my appreciating their role to a greater extent, coupled with my increased frustration in attempting to influence their abundance by management measures such as chemical treatment.

Besides the fact that many species of waterfowl eat aquatic plants, other animals in the water eat plants too. Crayfish eat all kinds of aquatic plants. Many species of insects which spend part or all of their lifetime in the water will eat plant leaves, as will certain fishes. Most of the time these herbivores will not reduce the plant growth in a pond enough to be apparent, but occasionally they will. A little water bug found in the part of the country where I live, has performed a dramatic reduction of Eurasian water milfoil in a few large, natural lakes.

The role of algae in the pond is a little different. Although they are most important primary converters of nutrients to usable form by small animal plankton, some forms can *really* be a nuisance. Especially enriched ponds may experience chronic problems with blue-green algaes. These algaes are not only a poor source of food for animal plankton, they may even contain toxins in their cells which can kill cattle that drink the water. Once a pond develops a blue-green algae abundance, it is difficult to control. Bluegreen algae can regulate their buoyancy, meaning that they may be seen at the water's surface, or may be on the pond bottom. Unfortunately, they also can out-compete desirable species of green algae.

Sometimes drastic measures, such as the dying off of the entire fish population, may lead to a change in animal plankton to much larger forms, which are more efficient at grazing on algae. Lakes and ponds where I have seen fish kills, in a few months a strong regrowth, or "pulse" of large, wriggly, clouds of organisms in the water usually follows. One may be assured that these organisms are forms of animal plankton, such as Daphnia, that are consuming algae as fast as they can and that can lead to a reduction of algae surpluses.

The biological fact of life is that populations of small fish, such as bluegills, like to feed on these larger animal plankton. Given enough mouths to feed in a pond, the bluegills can reduce these algae grazers sufficiently so that the algae may again become abundant. Hypothetically, a pond with no small bluegills is less likely to have an algae problem. I do not know whether I have looked at ponds and lakes exactly in this manner yet to confirm this hypothesis, although it may well be true. There are times when our pond was virtually devoid of fish and yet I continued to observe substantial growth of filamentous algae.

Usually, a variety of aquatic plants are present in our pond at any given time. However, in the past four years, the submergent plant growth has been dominated by water buttercup (Figure 35), and the emergent plant growth by cattails. Of course, many other species of plants continue to be present. However, for one to drive onto the dam, or take a canoe out onto the water, these two forms would be the most conspicuous, at least at times when mats of filamentous algae are not present at the surface.

Frequently, when one species of aquatic plant is nearly eliminated from the pond, another species will appear and may become abundant. This can happen because the controlled species was out-competing the second species and when it became absent, the second species was able to establish dominance. I have seen this happen a number of times. For example, when a species like curlyleaf pondweed became dense at the surface in early May and virtually shaded out other submergent plants. Once this canopy was removed, a species such as leafy pondweed may become conspicuous. The leafy pondweed may not have even been apparent up until that time.

In recent years, as I have said, two species of plants have pretty well established dominance in the scenery of the pond: cattails and water buttercup. The former is quite common in pond and lake margins in the midwest and other wetlands and the latter, water buttercup, is a somewhat unusual species. How it became so prolific in my pond is a mystery. It must be an ideal environment for this species (depth, pH, bottom soils). I can control it chemically, but often with dire consequences to the pond life (See Generalities about Chemical Control of Aquatic Plants).

The amount of plants present is a kind of index to productivity of water. The existence of seventeen pounds of larger (non-algae) aquatic plants is about equivalent to one pound of fish in some sort of strange, biological equation.

A couple of species of wetland plants that may be considered unusual, are bulrushes and liverworts. Bulrushes, a kind of scenic plant which reminds one of natural lakes (Figure 36 B), are not usually found around artificial ponds like ours. I have never seen liverworts (Figure 36), before finding them at the pond in 1992. The plant is flat and geometrically lobed, as can be seen in the picture taken of the one posing on a styrofoam cup.

A plant we *don't* want to see around the pond is the exotic purple loosestrife (Figure 37). It has come into our continent from Europe recently and tends to take over wetland areas, crowding out native plants. I have seen it mostly along ditches and marshes in northern Illinois, but have also heard of people planting it intentionally around their houses because it is a tall, bright, showy plant when in bloom. Take my advice: if you see it, get rid of it. Plant people are even now importing insect parasites which will feed specifically on purple loosestrife.

Generalities About Chemical Control of Aquatic Plants

After I had been chemically treating the algae and other plants in the pond for nine or ten consecutive years, a certain scenario

began to become apparent. The scenario is basically this:
1. Filamentous algae would appear early in the spring;
2. Treat the algae chemically and control would be temporary:
3. a. Filamentous algae would come back in two or three weeks and would require treatment again; or
   b. Rooted, submergent aquatic plants would appear in May and algae would not longer be abundant;
4. Treat the rooted, submergent plants chemically in May or June;
5. a. Plants would be only partially affected; or
   b. Rooted, submergent plants would disappear and algae would reappear at once. Dissolved oxygen in water would become low;
6. a. Rooted, submergent plants would again become abundant; or
   b. Abundant filamentous algae would be treated again, several times. Dissolved oxygen may get lower with each successive treatment; or
   c. Plankton algae may replace filamentous algae. Water color turns green and visibility becomes poor.

Whoa! Even a poor, dumb guy like me can figure this one out. If this is beginning to sound like a dead end track, you're right! While I was busy killing plants, I was creating temporarily unsatisfactory water quality conditions for other animals in my pond, like fish. At the same time, I was accelerating the deposit of a thick, black, organic sediment on the bottom of the pond, stuff which not only has a high demand for oxygen, but is also rich in nutrients, like phosphorus. This demand for oxygen may not cause a critical problem until next winter, under the ice, at which time it could bring about winterkill of aquatic creatures.

I'm afraid what I have described above is not only well documented for my own pond, but for what I have observed in many other nearby lakes and ponds during my forty-odd years as a working biologist. What one is doing when one makes a practice of chemical aquatic plant control is simply accelerating Mother Nature's time-line on eutrophication or enrichment. Along with this, one is throwing in occasionally spots of "poorer than normal" water quality as an added attraction. Having shallow water and fertile soils to begin with, exacerbates the situation.

Sometimes the smell of decomposition will come off the water within ten days after chemical plant treatment, particularly if it is algae which all seems to die at once. The smell indicates a drop in dissolved oxygen in the water. If one operates an aerator system in the pond at this time, as I have, it makes the smell more conspicuous, as the water circulation drives the gases resulting from the decomposition into the atmosphere. In face of this, the aerator may be unable to provide any additional oxygen to the water, and fish may suffocate in spite of it all.

Another nail in the coffin may be that if an algae abundance reappears, it may be a bluegreen species which has little food value to the small animal plankton which would ordinarily feed on other kinds of algae. This may temporarily short-circuit a major portion of the food chain for fish.

Mother Nature demands plant diversity, both on land and in the water. "Oh, what a tangled web we weave, when first we practice to deceive . . . (Mother Nature)".

Grass carp

From 1965 to 1988, I tried various kinds of chemicals in attempts to achieve reduction of aquatic plants and algae which sometimes grew extensively in the pond. About the year 1987, the use of an exotic, herbivorous fish known as the grass carp, or white amur, began to receive recognition in Illinois in the management of plants in lakes and ponds. This fish, originally brought to the USA from from Asia in 1963, became legal to introduce into Illinois waters but only in the triploid (hybrid) form so it could not reproduce.

Aquatic herbicides rarely gave long-term control of the target plant species. Besides that, the killing of aquatic plants often gave rise to other problems in the pond, (i.e.) low dissolved oxygen, buildup of organic material on the bottom, change from one kind of plant to another less desirable species, loss of use of the pond for whatever waiting period the chemical label directed and cost of purchase and application of the chemical. All these factors prompted me in 1988, to try biological control in the form of stocking grass carp. At the time, I had some prior experience with grass carp stockings in other lakes and ponds, but I had followed none of them long enough to be certain what the pros and cons were in the use of these fish. Initially, my experience with other bodies of water suggested that the grass carp did not always produce a noticeable reduction in the aquatic plant problem, at least in the first two to four years after their introduction.

In June of 1988, I stocked six triploid grass carp which were from 8 to 11 inches in length (Figure 38). The condition of these fish was good when stocked and I suspect they all survived the initial shock of stocking. Because there were larger bass and northern pike present in the pond at the time, it is possible that some of these fish may have been eaten within the first couple of months after stocking. Great blue herons also frequent the pond, and they are quite capable of catching and eating a fish of this size. It was necessary to chemically treat both leafy pondweed and algae in the pond a month after the grass carp stocking.

The first evidence of the survival of the grass carp came when our oldest son, Kevin, caught one on a tube jig and a piece of night crawler on September 5th of the same year. At this time, the fish had been in the pond only three months, and had already grown to nearly 18 inches in length. He returned this fish to the water. Incidentally, it is not very often that grass carp are caught on hook and line and this was the only time it occurred from my pond up to the present.

Leafy pondweed, slender naiad, some water buttercup and Illinois pondweed were growing in the pond during the early summer of 1989, the one-year presence of grass carp apparently not deterring plant abundance. I was afraid at this time that all the grass carp may have been eaten by predators, for other than the single fish my son had seen, no other grass carp had been observed during the year.

In 1990, chara, water buttercup and filamentous algae appeared early in the spring. Setting an experimental gill net in May did not result in catching any grass carp, reaffirming my suspicion that none might be left; however, on June 4th, while wearing sun glasses and paddling around in my canoe, I observed three grass carp swimming happily together near the surface. Their length appeared to be about 21 inches and I estimated their weight at nine pounds. At the same time, there was a substantial growth of chara, leafy pondweed and water buttercup in the pond, so the presence of the fish was not having a noticeable effect on the abundance of these three aquatic plant species. Supposedly, both chara and leafy pondweed are species which the grass carp prefer as food.

In the fish die-off which occurred in the pond in June of '90, caused by runoff of the insecticide *Counter* following heavy rainfall, no grass carp were among the fish carcasses. I saw a single, live, large grass carp on August 25, 1990.

Chara and water buttercup began growing strongly in the pond by May and June of 1991, along with a lot of filamentous algae. I saw two grass carp on June 16 and on August 8 and a single fish on September 4th. Their size was very large by then. Often they would give away their presence by loud splashing at the surface, especially when they were frightened.

In April of 1992, four years after the grass carp stocking, water buttercup again appeared in the pond and leafy pondweed, filamentous algae and a little chara appeared in May. I observed three grass carp together in shallow water in early September. They appeared to be about ten pounds in weight. Three grass carp were observed together several more times later in 1992, but never more than three. The evidence would suggest that only these three fish remained from the original stocking, and it would also suggest that this number of grass carp in my pond was insufficient to influence significantly the growth of aquatic plants, even if the plants are the kind which these fish like to eat. Later information developed on the use of grass carp to control aquatic plants, suggests that I should have stocked about 25-30 of these fish initially in our two acre, pond and should follow it five years later with another 25 grass carp.

It is possible that the grass carp have effected the chara growth in the pond as chara appeared to be significantly lower in abundance than it had been before 1988. I don't believe the grass carp have effected the abundance of leafy pondweed, water buttercup, or slender naiad, however.

Grass carp will usually graze the plants they like to eat down to soil level. Because large quantities of plant material are processed by their digestive systems, their feeding may actually increase levels of nitrates and phosphorus in the water simply by converting plantbound nutrients into more available fecal waste products.

Capturing grass carp in a pond or lake after they have been stocked is very difficult. Since stocking this species in our pond in 1988, I have sampled the fish population by pulling nets (100 foot seine), setting experimental mesh gill nets, and using electrofishing. With none of these sampling devices have I yet collected a grass carp; however, I occasionally have collected them in other lakes. The most common way of observing these fish is either from an elevated position along the shore, such as standing on the dam, or paddling around quietly in a canoe. They are a very "spooky" fish and readily "stampede" if they sense anyone to be nearby.

The final chapter in the lives of those remaining grass carp occurred in early June of 1993, when the pond experienced a die-off of fish, due to low dissolved oxygen. The fish carcasses I observed in June were all bass and bluegills. I didn't see any dead grass carp. After sampling the pond with several fish collection devices, I was not able to catch any live fish. Because of the very low dissolved oxygen present off and on from June through September, I assumed all the fish which had been present in the pond had died and their bodies decomposed, although in late June I saw a large swirl in the water which often betrays the presence of a grass carp.

In mid-August I could see the fresh carcasses of three large grass carp. They had probably died (Figure 38 B) a few days after I recently applied copper sulfate to kill back the filamentous algae, causing the dissolved oxygen to become even lower. These were the remaining grass carp in the pond and they had survived the low oxygen conditions which had killed all the bass and bluegills two months previously. These fish were now from 30 to 36 inches in length and probably weighed at least 15 pounds. Their carcasses floated at the surface for a period of more than two months before they finally decomposed sufficiently to sink. One could smell them a long distance away.

Conclusions one could draw from this specific experience with grass carp are:
1. Not all grass carp stocked at a size of 8 to 10 inches can be expected to live until the next year, especially if there are predator fish or fish-eating birds present.
2. Six grass carp is an insufficient stocking in a two acre pond to achieve any meaningful aquatic plant control, even if the plants are species which these fish prefer.
3. Grass carp will grow very rapidly . . . perhaps from an initial 1/4 pound to 15 pounds over four years.
4. This fish can survive relatively low dissolved oxygen conditions which may kill bass and other sunfishes, but will also die when oxygen gets extremely low, i.e. under 2 mg/L, for a prolonged period.
5. The species is very timid and may not be observed in the waters where stocked for some time afterwards. Approaching the pond slowly, wearing sunglasses, with the sunlight to my back was about the only way I could get to see them.

More recently, in June of 1994, I stocked 24 young grass carp in order to give a larger number of this species a chance of showing their stuff in controlling the aquatic plants in the pond. This is a density of 12 fish/acre and is more in line with current recommendations for the number of this fish needed to achieve aquatic plant control. It will probably require at least two years for me to evaluate how effective these fish may be, provided they don't die or get eaten by predators in the meantime. Even though I had no bass large enough to eat them in 1994, I did frequently see our old friend, the great blue heron, fishing at the pond off and on.

This second stocking of grass carp consisted of fish averaging ten inches in length. When I was able to see some of them next, three months later, swimming near the surface, they appeared to be about 14 or 15 inches in length. By October of that year, I was able to see fragments of leafy pondweed floating in the pond. This could have been an indication of the feeding on these plants by the grass carp, or maybe by the geese and mallards which were also present on the pond in October. These waterfowl also like to pull up aquatic plants. Biological equations are rarely very simple.

Insects

Aquatic insects

Anyone who hangs around a pond or lake for very long can tell of experiences with insects. Many of these insects originate as a result of the body of water, such as mosquitoes and dragonflies. One can also see the whirlygig beetles at the surface on a calm day, dodging around in their busy little circles. We had a standing joke about these little groups of whirlygigs whenever we were working on a lake. The night before it would be: "Who's going to get up first in the morning and go down and wind up the whirlygig beetles?" Another surface insect, but not quite so conspicuous, is the water strider. It is known to some as the Jesus bug, because of its ability to walk on the surface tension of the water with its feet. It looks much like a large mosquito, but without the sting.

Those insects which spend a part of their life cycle in the water, are also very important to fish. Fish like bluegills, eat many kinds of these little water animals all of their lives. Channel catfish may eat the insects and larvae which are burrowed in the mud. Largemouth bass may eat insects, when the bass is a juvenile, or are smaller than ten inches.

I found that one of the best ways to tell what kinds of aquatic insects are in my pond is simply to look inside the stomachs of bluegills which we just caught. The insects eaten by bluegills are mostly the life phases that live in the water, like larvae and nymphs. As adults, the insects species may emerge from the water and fly away, or may continue to hang around the water and possibly be eaten as an adult by a fish, or by a bird that may skim along the surface of the pond, like a swallow.

For me, it is difficult to identify many of the early life stages of insect larvae and nymphs which I find in a bluegill's stomach, although I do know a few. Fortunately, I had a friend, Leka Jovanovic, who is good at this, so frequently I asked him to do it for me. Following is a kind of laundry list of different insects found. I'm giving you this list, not to confuse you, because you also will recognize a lot of these insects. I list them because it shows some of the variety of life within a pond which one fish may ingest:

 Dragonflies   Water fleas
 Damsel flies   Daphnia
 Mayflies   Midges
 Mosquitoes (biting and non-biting)

The adult dragonflies (Figures 39, 39 B) and their miniature version, the damsel flies, are very colorful. Species may range from a metallic green to a chrome yellow in color. Besides the insects, there are other animals and plants frequently found in the bluegill's stomach:

 Snails and clams   Filamentous algae
 Leeches   Plant fragments

I've got a suspicion that some of the algae and other plants may get into the bluegill's stomach when it is foraging for aquatic animals on the plants, and it gets a little salad along with them, inadvertently.

The abundance of aquatic insects is greater in a lake or a pond like mine, when rooted, submergent, aquatic plants are present. This is because the plants provide both shelter and food for the insects and for other animals too, like snails, crayfish and clams (Figure 40). Abundance of this sort of life may be ten times greater in areas of plants than it is in open water. This is a matter to remember when one gets over-enthusiastic about the control of aquatic plant growth.

The other day I saw a male water beetle stroking his way through shallow water and carrying a load of eggs on his back which his loving mate had deposited there for him to babysit. This large beetle can eat fish, besides being eaten by fish. I also saw a lot of "pill" clams clinging to the water buttercup plants under water. Their name is appropro, as they are about the same size as the 1/4 inch diameter pills I take every day for cholesterol.

The swarms of little flies which like to get into your eyes when riding a bicycle, or to dot up the windshield of your car, are most likely midges. The midges originate from tiny, red, worm-like larvae living in the mud in the bottom of a pond like mine. Some may come from streams. At first, you may believe you've been attacked by mosquitoes, but soon you find out they're not biting. They are one of the most important food items of young fish, although they digest so rapidly in a fish's stomach, you may not see them there.

The innocent little black and white backswimmer is one you want to beware of when you're playing around in the water. This one can and will enjoy inflicting a painful sting on your bare flesh. This has happened to me more than once while I was sorting through plants and fish that I was collecting from the water.

Other kinds of very tiny animal life, besides insects, which one is bound to find in a pond or lake, are called "zooplankton". The best way to look for these little animals in a pond is to bring a mason jar full of pond water back into your house and hold it up to the light. If all goes normally, you will see little life forms darting around within the water column. These are the zooplankton, which like algae are the basis of the food chain for all larger aquatic animals. They are the converters of plant energy to animal energy and you can see them in the water in the winter as well as in the summer.

The abundance of "critters" like aquatic insects and snails that are hanging onto submerged plants becomes obvious to anyone swimming among the plants, with SCUBA gear. Also, simply pulling out the plants and rinsing them off in a white pail will shake off numbers that you never imagined were there . . . even more than get on you when you lie down on your lawn.

Chronicle of a Pesticide Fish Kill

Within the forty acre watershed to the pond lies about a five acre portion of a cultivated field on our farm. This five acres slopes gently toward the pond and ends about fifty feet from the pond's edge at a grassy strip and lane around the east side (Figure 41). During heavy rainfall runoff, this part of the field can wash water and sediment into the pond. Light rainfalls will not do this.

In mid-May of 1987, this cultivated field was planted with corn, and a nematacide with the trade name of "Counter", a systemic insecticide, was applied to the field at a rate of 8 lbs/ acre, for control of corn root worm. Also, a herbicide called "Atrazine" was applied at the same time. *Counter,* an organophosphate (Terbufos), is known for its toxicity to animals. For that matter, insecticides are generally much more toxic to warm-blooded animals and aquatic life than are herbicides, some by several orders of magnitude. The common agricultural selective herbicide *Atrazine,* may also be toxic, but by many orders *less* so than the insecticide Counter.

The week following the application of the chemicals, three inches of rainfall occurred in the space of a few days, and water carrying considerable sediment drained off from the five acre portion of this treated cultivated field, into the pond. By May 21st,

I could see a few dead bluegills, mostly of small size, floating at the pond surface, and by May 23rd, I could count nearly a thousand dead bluegills and ten dead bass at the surface (Figure 42), while paddling around the pond in my canoe. Although I could smell the decomposition of the fish carcasses and the water color had become tannish, my tests of the dissolved oxygen in the pond water showed it was still adequate to maintain fish life. I had been operating the aerator in the pond for several days. The water temperature at this time was 56°F. In addition, there was a disproportionately higher number of bluegills among the dead fish, about 100 bluegills to each bass. This suggested to me that the toxicity was selective, i.e., that whatever was killing the fish was more toxic to bluegills than to bass.

Another feature in this event was the matter that before this fish kill had occurred, there was a heavy growth of filamentous algae in the pond, the pond surface being nearly half covered with the growth. Following the fish kill, the algae diminished by about 70%. This may have been due to the herbicide Atrazine, which also must have washed into the pond from the cornfield. The many small pieces of organic material which I could see floating in the water, could come from both the dead fish and dead algae.

On May 25th, my son Peter and I pulled a 30 foot long seine in the pond and got no live fish, but ended up with a lot of black, stinky, organic gunk in the net. A gill net set the same day, however, caught three lively bass and one northern pike, all apparently in good condition. It appeared to me that practically all the aquatic insects in the pond were dead, however snails, leeches and tadpoles were alive. Five schools of newly hatched bass fry were seen the next day.

Summary

After checking into the toxicity of the chemical terbufos (Counter), I found that it is toxic to bluegills at a rate of 1.7 ppb (parts per billion or ug/Kg). This is several times more toxic than the chemical (5% rotenone), which is used by fishery biologists when they intentionally want to kill fish in waters. It is also highly toxic to humans, both orally and through the skin. The herbicide Atrazine, on the other hand, is low in toxicity to humans.

What apparently happened in the pond was that there was sufficient Counter washed off the cornfield into the pond, to kill most of the bluegills and aquatic insects. Enough Atrazine also washed into the pond to kill some of the algae. A formulation of Atrazine, called Aquazine, has been sold for some time as an aquatic herbicide. Decomposition of the fish and algae reduced the dissolved oxygen in the water somewhat, but not enough to cause suffocation of fish. Following the reduction of filamentous algae (the mossy-looking stuff), the planktonic (pea-soup) algae became much more abundant. This could have been a result of the release of nutrients and growth of bacteria, following the decomposition of all the fish carcasses in the water.

I took a sediment sample from the pond bottom on May 26th, to analyze for Counter; however, it could not be detected at the level of laboratory capability (50 ug/Kg). Because this chemical breaks down in time in the presence of alkaline water and sunlight, it was apparently undetectable five days after the fish kill; however laboratory detection limits for minimum limits were not sufficient to rule out toxic levels. There was substantial survival of all species of fish in the pond, so I did not restock it with any additional fish. I did, however, prohibit fishing in the pond for several months because I was afraid of the edibility of the fish to humans. Subsequently, many additional small, dead snails washed up on shore.

An interesting aspect of this heavy die-off of bluegills is that later in the year bluegills of unusually large size were being caught by fishermen, particularly through the ice in the following winter and in open water in the spring of 1988, at which time some bluegills larger than eight or nine inches were caught—a rare phenomenon. I think the two factors responsible for this were: (1.) A much larger proportion of smaller bluegills were killed by the chemical, leaving mostly larger fish and, (2.) The remaining bluegills grew at a substantially faster rate, due to the lack of competition for food, even though their forage of aquatic insects had been temporarily reduced by the same chemical.

In the month that followed this fish kill, many of the bass and bluegills which remained alive in the pond showed split or frayed fins, perhaps a result of stress. Fishing for bass was quite good later in the year. Apparently the bass also lacked a lot of their usual forage (small bluegills) and were willing to hit anything the fisherman threw at them.

As an outgrowth of the fish kill, I asked the farmers, Elmer and Jim, who rented our cropland, to refrain from using the chemical Counter again and to use something less toxic if corn rootworm control was felt necessary. The label on the *Counter* chemical bag states that the product is toxic to fish, birds and other wildlife, and not to apply near water or wetlands. Also, that runoff may be hazardous to aquatic organisms in neighboring areas. In McHenry County where our farm is located, there are a number of ponds and lakes. The county is also interlaced with streams and ditches. It is likely that most cornfields would drain within a short distance into a water area where aquatic life is present, and that this life would presumably be placed in jeopardy by any runoff from treated land occurring shortly after the application of this pesticide. I cannot find definitive information on how long it takes this chemical to break down and lose its toxicity after it is applied to the soil.

Later, in talking with a local veterinarian, he recounted several instances with which he was familiar where domestic animals had been injured or killed as a result of contact with Counter. Toxicity tests show that skin toxicity to rabbits is 1.1 mg/kg and that it can be absorbed through the skin. This emphasizes that this chemical is extremely poisonous.

I suspect that a die-off of about thirty small bluegills and one northern pike, which had occurred exactly one year earlier in my pond, was also due to the use of Counter on the same cornfield. A modest rainfall runoff had also happened shortly after that application of the chemical, but not nearly as much runoff as in 1987. How long after application of this chemical to fields does it represent a hazard to aquatic life from rainfall runoff, I do not know; however, the fact that it has been a commonly used nematacide on corn land in the midwest, suggests that accidents of this sort may occur more frequently than we suspect.

Light mortality of fish was also noted in May of 1991, involving a few bass and a channel catfish. I had measured dissolved oxygen regularly through the winter in the pond, so the die-off was not due to low oxygen as one might initially suspect. Because Counter was not used as a pesticide on the nearby corn field the prior year, I suspect that in this instance the herbicide Atrazine may have been involved. Atrazine is highly soluble and tends to escape with rainfall runoff. It is one of the most common agricultural chemicals found in well water. It may be more toxic to aquatic life than to warm-blooded animals, but I have yet found no literature which allows this comparison.

One can sample the soils in fields and the water in ponds for a variety of commonly used agricultural pesticides. One series, called the Nitrogen Phosphorus Detector (NPD) analysis, tests for a dozen different pesticides of soil or water, and costs about $200.00. Early collection of the sample following pesticide application is necessary, as some of the compounds may deteriorate rapidly in the presence of rainfall and sunlight.

Much of the data in this discussion of pesticide properties comes from: *Farm Chemicals Handbook, '92,* 1992. Meister Publishing Company, Willoughby, Ohio. One may also call the National Pesticides Telecommunication Network (1-800-858-PEST) and get instant, free information on the toxicity of pesticides and herbicides. Their information comes mainly off the EPA Pesticide Fact Sheet, dated September 9, 1988.

Chronicle of a Herbicide Fish Kill

By early June of 1990, several species of rooted, submergent aquatic plants were appearing in shallow water—less than five feet deep. Most abundant was leafy pondweed, along with water buttercup and Illinois pondweed. Chara was also growing in the south part of the pond. This latter species, chara, is really a form of higher algae attached to the bottom and is the most dense in its growth, achieving a great mass of weight, but rarely extending beyond five feet of water depth in our pond.

Because the abundance of submerged plants interferes both with the recreational use of the pond and also with our ability to pull a small net through shallow water for fish studies, I chose to apply a plant control chemical in the limited area of the beach location. This is about 1/8th of the area of the entire pond. Hydrothol 191 (endothall), made by Pennwalt, is effective in controlling both leafy pondweed and chara, so I sprayed one gallon over an area of about one-quarter acre around the beach. I have used this contact herbicide before in other locations and knew from experience that it does not take much to reach toxic levels for fish. The label application rate is suggested at 1-3 gallons of liquid 191 per acre-foot of water. The label also states that fishing not be allowed for three days following application of this chemical. I decided that to be on the safe side, I would apply only one gallon to this limited area of the pond. The entire volume of the pond is 8 acre-feet.

Immediately prior to application, I noted that bluegills were on their spawning nests, but bass were not. I diluted the chemical 30 to one with water and sprayed it over the surface from my boat on June 12th. I turned on the pond aerator immediately after applying the chemical, and noted that there was an odor from the disturbed water, indicating that the pond had been thermally stratified, and that there was probably little dissolved oxygen in the deeper water. This odor comes from gases resulting from organic decomposition occurring in deeper water, and the action of the aerator circulates the deep water to the surface, where the gases and the odor may escape.

The next day I looked at the treated area in the pond, and could observe that the chara was already showing a wilting effect from the chemical, and that the water had turned a tannish color. Leafy pondweed and Illinois pondweed also looked dead in the treated area. A few small, dead fish could be seen at the surface, mostly yearling bass and bluegills, and all confined to the area where I had sprayed the day before. Plants and fish outside the treated area appeared unaffected; however, the aerator was still running, and the smell of decomposition that I had noticed before still persisted. In examination of the dissolved oxygen in the water, I found 7.4 mg/L at a depth of two feet. Anything above 3.5 mg/L would be considered a safe level for warm water fish and other aquatic life.

That same evening a heavy rain began and after 12 hours, it culminated in a total of five inches of rainfall in the pond's watershed. A great volume of runoff water entered the pond and overflowed the spillway. Water transparency dropped from being very clear to only five inches of visibility, due to the volume of soil sediment being carried into the pond from the five acre cultivated portion of the watershed.

I didn't go down to the pond until two days later, after my son-in-law, John, told me he saw numerous dead fish there. I assumed he meant the same small fish I had seen the day after treatment. When I looked at the pond, I saw a lot of fish bodies of all sizes floating at the surface (Figure 43). I also saw a twelve inch bass which was in distress, at the surface. On this day, I counted the following dead fish:

Largemouth bass — 12 to 15 inches (42)
" " 6 to 11 inches (60)
" " 3 to 5 inches (75)
Bluegill — 7 to 9 inches (45)
" 4 to 6 inches (92)
" 2 to 3 inches (about 500)

No dead northern pike nor grass carp were seen.

Visibility in the water was still reduced to five inches due to suspended sediment. I took a dissolved oxygen test at a depth of one foot and it was 3.4 mg/L, indicating a critically low level. Carcasses of fish lying on the pond bottom did not become visible until they bloated and rose to the surface.

Two days later (seven days after treatment), I visited the pond again. The aerator had been off for awhile due to an electrical outage, but had come back on again after several hours. By this time, the fish carcasses had floated mostly into shallow water and were hung up among the cattails. I could see no live fish. Water visibility had improved to 12 inches, but at one foot of depth, the dissolved oxygen was only 1.8 mg/L. Water was still flowing actively over the spillway.

Although the water still retained some of its clay color nine days after herbicide treatment, the visibility had improved 30 inches. Dissolved oxygen remained critically low, with 1.2 mg/L at one foot deep and 0.8 mg/L at three feet. No live fish were observable in the pond, nor around the entrance of the tile water to the pond, where the dissolved oxygen was 7.2 mg/L. I collected 25 of the larger bass carcasses and dumped them on the other side of the spillway. This would represent about 1/3 of the large bass which had died. I did not attempt to pick up many of the bluegills, which ranged from 2-9 inches in length. I estimate the total weight of dead bluegills to be about three times that of the dead bass. This would come close to being the true proportion of the total weight of living bluegills to bass under normal conditions, I believe. A strong odor of dead fish remained.

There was a lot of suspended organic matter in the water, and the clay sediment, which had been visible throughout the water column, was now settled out on the bottom of the pond. Even though there were still living aquatic plants remaining, including leafy pondweed, water buttercup and chara, there was apparently enough decomposition going on to overcome any dissolved oxygen production by these living plants. Clumps of dead chara could be seen floating at the surface and a bluegreen algae associated with decomposition, was also present at the surface in globs. The aerator was off for 24 hours, but when running for several days, it hadn't been able to overcome the low dissolved oxygen.

Twenty days (T + 20) following the plant treatment, the foul odor was no longer apparent around the pond and the fish carcasses had all disappeared. Water visibility was reduced back down to fifteen inches. The dissolved oxygen had risen to 17 mg/L at one foot, 10 mg/L at three feet, and 1.3 mg/L at five feet of depth. The water color was a dirty-grey. It appeared that the algae present in the upper waters was providing ample dissolved oxygen; however in the deeper water, where sunlight cannot penetrate, the dissolved oxygen remained low. I could still see no live fish. Some strands of water buttercup were still living; however I saw clumps of leafy pondweed floating at the surface. Some of the chara on the bottom was still green, but it was sparse.

Twenty-two days after treatment (T + 22) the greenish color to the water indicated a strong plankton algae growth was present. Visibility in the water had improved to 27 inches. The aerator had been operating for twelve hours, and dissolved oxygen was now present in substantial amounts, from the surface to the bottom in nine feet of water. My son and I made two hauls with a 30 foot, 1/4 inch mesh seine and collected, to my surprise and delight, one lively twelve inch bass in apparently healthy condition, but no other fish. A lot of living aquatic insects were present in our seine hauls, including dragonfly and diving beetle larvae.

Three days later (T + 25) we made several more seine hauls, but captured no additional live fish. However, many living diving beetles and backswimmers were present among the aquatic insects. Decomposed organic material was still floating at the pond's surface, even though individual plants of water buttercup and chara could be seen alive.

On July 9th (T + 29) a strong growth of green, plankton algae was evident, promoting substantial dissolved oxygen from the surface down to five feet of depth. The aerator, which had been operating for six days, was distributing the dissolved oxygen more evenly from top to bottom. I saw the swirl of a large fish which was probably a grass carp. A lot of dead snails could be seen around the pond's edge.

On July 14th, Pete and I pulled a 50 foot bag seine two times. We did not get any fish, but did get a lot of mucky, organic matter in the net.

By July 23rd (T + 43), with the aerator off for two weeks, the dissolved oxygen had again stratified markedly, with high oxygen in surface water down to about four feet deep, and very little in water deeper than that. This corresponds quite well with the depth of sunlight penetration, so the growth of plankton algae in the upper water was providing that layer with a lot of dissolved oxygen. Shading of sunlight and a high rate of decomposition in deeper water was still depleting oxygen there, where no mixing is occurring from operation of the aerator. In shallow water, leafy pondweed and Illinois pondweed was present; however there was no aquatic vegetation growing in water greater than three feet deep.

July 28 (T + 49) The aerator had been turned on for two days and had caused an equalization of dissolved oxygen in the water column. However, even though there was an adequate amount of dissolved oxygen down to eight feet deep, it was still much below saturation, meaning that the water at this temperature could hold a lot more dissolved oxygen. This demonstrates that there was high biochemical oxygen demand caused by decomposition in the bottom material. Living leafy pondweed had become abundant again in certain locations in the pond. I shut the aerator off.

July 30 (T + 51) With the aerator off for two days, the dissolved oxygen had again markedly stratified in the water column, with a lot in the upper waters and very little in deep water. The visibility had improved to 34 inches, which is about what average conditions would be for the month of July. The water was virtually alive with tiny backswimmers. Apparently there had been a good hatch of these insects in the past month and there were few predators present to eat them.

August 8 (T + 60) The aerator had been off for eleven days and there was adequate dissolved oxygen down to five feet deep, but not much below this. Plankton algae was still apparent near the surface. On this date I could see many young fish in shallow water, which appeared to be bass. Their small size indicated they probably hatched out in the past six weeks, which would be *after* the fish die-off. There had to be at least one pair of adult bass survive in the pond.

Summary of the fish kill

By mid-June, the pond is ordinarily becoming stratified with its dissolved oxygen, that is, it has adequate dissolved oxygen from the surface down to six or seven feet deep, but little oxygen in the deepest water. This is the time of year that excessive growth of rooted, submergent aquatic plants, or floating algae, also occurs.

Prior chemical treatments of aquatic plants that I have done, usually resulted in further depletion of dissolved oxygen in the water due to an accelerated decomposition of the plants. Several critical factors come into play in determining how poor the water conditions may become: (1.) The density of the plants that decompose; (2.) How rapidly they decompose: (3.) The water temperature during decomposition; (4.) How much sunlight there may be in the days immediately following treatment; and (5.) Any other climatic factors, such as sediment runoff in rainfall, that may further reduce dissolved oxygen.

In the instance of this fish kill there was a minor fish die-off initially, confined to the area I had applied the chemical, which I attribute directly to the toxicity of the particular chemical I used to kill the plants. Chara, the principal plant present at the time of treatment, had achieved a high density and was mostly killed by the treatment. This presented a large, decomposing mass within three days.

An unusually heavy rainfall accompanied by sediment runoff from the watershed and high turbidity in the pond occurred within 48 hours of treatment. This further reduced dissolved oxygen, which was already under stress from the decomposing plants. Dissolved oxygen in shallow water had been adequate before the rainfall runoff occurred.

Several days of overcast weather followed the treatment, reducing the amount of oxygen production by algae, through limiting photosynthesis. Dissolved oxygen from June 15 to June 21, was reduced to less than fish would require (3 mg/L) for respiration. Dissolved oxygen returned to adequate levels by the first of July, aided to a great extent by vigorous growth of plankton algae in the upper water where sunlight was adequate.

Operating the aerator during the days of heaviest plant decomposition was not adequate to maintain oxygen for fish life, even though I found out later, some fish *had* survived. For a period of 17 days following the fish kill, it appeared that there were no live fish remaining. At that time, several hauls with a seine came up with one lively adult bass. Swirls of live fish at the surface were seen five days later, possibly from grass carp. By August 2nd, a school of young fish, which had recently hatched out, proved to be small largemouth bass. Some successful spawning had occurred following the fish kill.

By August 25th, more than two months after the fish kill, I could verify that some bass and at least one grass carp had survived; however, I had yet to find any living bluegills. As a consequence, I began stocking some adult bluegills into the pond in September.

Additional Herbicide Fish Kill

In July of 1995, five years after the fish kill described above, there was considerable density of water buttercup in shallower water and coontail in deeper water. At the surface of the water, there was also a lot of floating, filamentous algae. July 8th, I applied two gallons of Aquathol K (an endothall) and two gallons of Cutrine Plus (a copper derivative algacide). I broadcast these diluted herbicides with a hand dipper over selected areas of the pond. At this time, the pond was nearly full of water and my tests showed there to be adequate dissolved oxygen from the surface to the bottom. The aerator was operating on this date.

On July 11th, three days later, I collected live and healthy small bass and bluegills from a trap I had set. On July 15th, dissolved oxygen was still adequate at midday, even though the aerator had shut itself off for a day due to power outage. About 15% of the water buttercup had died from the chemical treatment of a week ago, and much of the algae had died back. The water had a tannish color, suggesting organic decomposition was going on. I turned the aerator back on and I saw a fish that looked like a grass carp swirl in open water.

When I went down to the pond on July 18th (T + 10), it was apparent that there had been a fish kill. Among the dead fish I counted 28 bass (9 to 13 inches in length), 43 bluegills (3 to 9 inches), two 19 inch grass carp, and one 17 inch channel catfish. Oddly, almost all of the fish were larger adults with few small fish carcasses seen. Small bluegills and bass under four inches, were seen alive here and there and were not gasping for air at the surface. Dissolved oxygen in the water tested between 4.3 and 4.7 mg/L at four o'clock in the afternoon, which is adequate to maintain fish life; however, water temperatures for the past several days had been unusually warm (80°F).

Over the next 24 hours, I conducted daytime and nighttime dissolved oxygen tests. I found that in the early morning, at 5 a.m., the dissolved oxygen was only between 0.9 and 1.5 mg/L. This is insufficient to maintain fish life; however by noon the dissolved oxygen had risen to 3.3 to 4.6 mg/L. The time the dissolved oxygen had been depressed was apparently too short a period on this date to kill the small fish which remained in the pond, as these fish remained lively when it was light enough to see them.

What had happened is what is called "night-time respiration". This is nothing unusual, because when light is no longer available for photosynthesis by plants, oxygen is not produced and the dissolved oxygen concentration progressively drops during the night. In this instance, the decomposition of the plants I had killed caused an excessive oxygen demand in the water, so that oxygen was somewhat low even during the day and got critically low at night. No doubt the fish that had died did so during the night. The puzzle remains though, why did only large fish die and almost no smaller ones when their oxygen requirements are almost identical? The unusually high water temperatures aggravated the situation, as warmer water cannot hold as much dissolved oxygen as cooler water.

By July 28th (T + 20), the dissolved oxygen had recuperated and was adequate from then on, both day and night. Tests with trap nets showed a substantial population of small bass and bluegills, under four inches, to exist; however I could find absolutely *no* larger fish even though I used seines, trap nets and gill nets. Were the number of carcasses of larger fish that I counted all there were in the pond? I doubt it. I think a lot of the dead fish were also lying on the pond bottom, out of my sight. Also, the pond was being visited often by several herons which would be interested in eating any floating fish they could get hold of, not to mention the feeding by adventurous raccoons which were also active at night around the shallow water.

Summary of this fish kill

This additional fish kill was caused by my application of two herbicides, one for rooted, submergent plants and one for algae. The kill was not caused by direct toxicity of the herbicides to the fish, as the application rates were much too low for this. Rather, it was a result of the decomposition of the plants in the water, removing too much of the dissolved oxygen, that resulted in suffocation of the fish. The actual suffocation no doubt occurred on one or two critical nights, when the plants which were still living were in respiration. The kill took out all of the larger fish, but few of the smaller bass and bluegills. It eliminated every channel catfish and grass carp, all of which were large fish.

The pond has so far not been restocked with any additional fish fourteen months following the kill. I may wish to see what the growth and survival is like among the surviving small bass and bluegills. Considerable growth was apparent by the end of October of the same year.

I believe that the build-up of additional organic matter to the bottom of the pond with each passing year, makes it more likely that fish kills like this one will occur in the future. Anything I do which depletes dissolved oxygen. like killing aquatic plants during warm weather, can bring about critical oxygen conditions in the water. This is because there is now a latent oxygen demand in the rich, black bottom muds, which is added to any other freshly decomposing organic material. Removing this rich mud would be nice to do, but would be very expensive. Some shallow areas of mud do become subject to more complete oxidation when these areas become exposed to air and sunlight, during periods of low water. This condition frequently occurs in the late summer and fall in our pond. Running the aerator in deeper water may also help somewhat to relieve this condition.

Chapter 6

Animals In and Around the Pond

Reptiles and Amphibians

To describe the snakes which we have seen around the pond is very simple. In two words, it is *garter snakes*. I have seen no other kind of snake within 500 feet of the pond. Garter snakes have been fairly common. I often see them when I turn over the canoe, lift up a board, or occasionally run over one with the mower. I recall seeing only one swimming in our pond, but I have seen them swimming elsewhere. In addition, I saw one dangling from the beak of a redtail hawk. The hawk was floating its way up to the top limb of an oak tree to enjoy his dessert, no doubt.

The description of the turtles we have observed is almost as simple. It is primarily the painted turtles, and they are common during the warm months. From October through March, I don't see them at all (earliest was March 29th). These turtles are frequently observed basking in the sun on any object which sticks up above the water and is strong enough to support them. I rarely have seen the painted turtle any distance from the pond, and I assume they hibernate in the pond mud during cold weather. They are a middle-size and somewhat colorful turtle, with an upper shell length of about five inches. I did once take a turtle out of the stomach of a two pound bass. It was about four to five inches in diameter across the shell. It had been slightly digested, but from the colors which I could see, it looked like a spotted turtle.

On rare occasions, maybe five or six times, I have also seen snapping turtles, either coming to or leaving the pond overland. Most recently I saw a big snapper in September (Figure 44). The few I have seen have all been quite large, and they appear to have no problem with traveling long distances overland, to get from one body of water to another. Baby snappers are miniatures of the adults and may be seen as small as golfball size. To say they are simply homely would be a compliment. Snappers are a little temperamental, but a person would need to go out of their way in carelessness in order to be bitten by one. You can be sure that the snapping turtle will not be afraid of you. The stew or soup made of snapping turtle meat is good—at least I like it. Snapping turtles, when looking for a free meal, are not above the trick of pulling ducks down below the surface by grabbing their feet from underneath.

While I am not certain, I believe the toads I see near the pond and occasionally in it, are all the American toad. I have never seen one that is large, but they all sport a lot of big warts and a spotted chest. They are often seen at the same time and place as leopard frogs (Figure 44 B) and the smaller chorus frogs (which are quite common), both in the water and in the grass within thirty feet of the water's edge. Unlike the toad, the leopard frog is difficult to catch and will squawk when you finally get hold of it. The American toad does not restrict his habitat to the pond, for I find them so frequently in our farmhouse basement that they are no longer a surprise to either me or my wife.

Also seen at the pond in the past few years have been bullfrogs (Figure 45). Bullfrogs and other frogs increased in abundance after the pond sustained two severe fish kills. Many hundreds of the tadpole stage of these frogs were seen before any adults. Whether this increase in frogs is due to a lack of fish predators, or whether it was coincidental, I do not know. I do know that in the year following a fish kill, the frogs became brave enough to float at the surface anywhere in the pond. They did *not* do this when larger bass were present. I have not yet seen a very large bullfrog, however I believe it takes several years for them to become large in size. We hear the deep, powerful call of the male, "Jug-o-rum", on occasion. The bullfrogs in the pond show a bright green jaw and yellow throat. Neither the adult nor tadpole bullfrogs have hibernated by the end of October, even though there had been several frosts before then.

In the late winter or early spring the first reptile or amphibian one is likely to see or hear around a lake or pond is a frog.

Chorus frogs can be seen on a warm day in March, jumping into water from shore when there is only four or five feet of open water out to the edge of the ice. The last time I saw this on our pond, it was March 14th of this year. In 1994 and 1995, bullfrogs became abundant. Coinciding with this, other frog and toad species have nearly disappeared. Adult bullfrogs are quite aggressive and will simply eat any other animal near the pond that they can catch, and which will fit in their mouths. Like Godzilla, they're not choosy. Of course, the bullfrog gets his comeuppance when there are larger bass in the pond, turning the tables to make the bullfrog the prey instead of the predator. In nature, turnabout is always fair play.

Although it is known that predator fish like bass eat frogs, I have never found a tadpole (Figure 46) in all the many bass stomachs I have examined. This may be because the tadpoles digest too rapidly. During the number of years I have handled frogs down at the pond, I have yet to see one that was deformed. Recently news media attention has given space to frogs with extra legs and eyes found in Minnesota and other states, suggesting the presence of unusual toxins in the environment. This could be a legitimate concern, so I'm going to pay more particular attention to our amphibious friends in the future.

Warmblooded Animals

Just a couple of mentions of warmblooded animals which are typically found around the pond, like the muskrat and the raccoon. The muskrat is often seen during the daytime, usually swimming across the pond and often with some kind of plant trailing from its mouth. Muskrats love our pond and the variety of plants which are present. They were able to find the pond within three years after it was constructed. Some of my farmer friends say they can come through tile lines; maybe so, but I'm certain they can also travel overland as witness a few road-kills I have seen. This rodent likes to dig holes in the shoreline, banks, and in the dam near the waterline. It will also sometimes build houses out of vegetation, like cattails, within the pond itself. These

Figure 46. Two species of tadpole.

Figure 47. Baby raccoon at night.

Figure 48. Son with deer.

Figure 50. Nesting box in pond.

Figure 51. D.U. nesting box.

Figure 52. Wood duck in tree.

Figure 53. Screech owl in D.U. box.

Figure 54. Hole in channel catfish.

Figure 55. Redwing blackbird.

Figure 56. Redwing nest and eggs.

Figure 57. Crayfish.

Figure 58. Stocking small bass and bluegills.

Figure 59. Six-inch one year old bass.

Figure 60. Bluegill spawning nest exposed.

Figure 61. Nine-inch bluegill.

Figure 62. Cloverleaf fish trap.

"hills" of cattails are around five to ten feet in diameter, and stick up above the surface of the water from one to three feet. Wildlife people say they build these houses as a source of food for the winter. We have watched muskrats nibbling off cattails at the waterline.

I suspect most pond owners would prefer their muskrats in the form of a fur coat. This is because of this rodent's pesky habit of digging holes which people and machinery frequently fall into. In some dams and dikes which are not very thick, muskrat holes may lead to leakage. Special designs in construction are needed to protect from this happening, such as rock rip-rap near the water line and metal flanges on pipes which pass through the dam. Fortunately, I had such barriers, called anti-seep collars, placed on my overflow pipe when it was laid through the dam. As for rock rip-rap along the face of the dam, we have been placing both field stones and broken concrete above and below the waterline on the dam, for a number of years. This slows down the muskrat excavations and the shoreline wave erosion to some extent, but I still have a lot more rocks to place before the dam is fully protected. A hydraulic scoop mounted on the tractor helps a lot, but "Oh, my aching back!".

Another problem muskrats have caused is their particular fondness for eating holes in the plastic aerator lines which we have placed on the pond's bottom. This is discussed further under the section entitled, *"Aerators and Aeration"*. I have yet to see any muskrat damages to our nearby young trees, however.

Perhaps the biggest predator on muskrats is the mink. We see mink once in a great while, but are more likely to see their tracks in the snow or in the mud around the pond's edge. Finding pieces of muskrat skeleton lying around with the flesh cleaned off the bones is a good clue to mink presence.

Like the mink, only rarely have I seen a living, breathing raccoon around the pond during the daytime. We see so many fresh tracks in the mud near the pond's edge, that it is obvious they are very busy catching frogs and crayfish there at night (Figure 47). We have a neighbor, Irv Schirmer, who likes to trap, so I let him trap muskrats and raccoons during the season. He gets from two to fifteen muskrats, and at least a couple of raccoons every season, depending upon their abundance. His zeal for fur trapping is in proportion to the prices he receives in a given year. In 1995, in the first five days of the trapping season, he had already caught five raccoons (at $13.00 per pelt). Not to worry about depleting the populations of these two species as there always seems to be more for next year. Raccoons like to use our barn in the wintertime. They play with and move everything that's moveable, in addition to leaving piles of their feces here and there on the horizontal wooden beams. This may be O.K., unless you prefer to have clean hay.

Some words of caution about the animals which one may find dead around the pond or farm: there are several diseases which can effect fox, rabbits, muskrats and/or raccoons and may cause fatalities to them. Some are contagious to other animals, but usually not to man. If you find a dead animal, bag it up while wearing gloves and bury it, or call your county health officer about its disposition.

Perhaps the most attractive animal seen at the pond is the whitetail deer. It is unusual when one can sneak up to the pond with sufficient stealth to catch a deer in view, but we do see many deer tracks, both adult and fawn, next to and out into the pond. Why they would like to step into and walk through the soft pond mud, I don't know. Often they do this even though there are plenty of other sources of water to drink. Possibly they browse on some of the aquatic plants, as many of them are edible and utilized by deer as forage, according to botanists.

The two willow-grown wetlands above and below the pond, which were a by-product of the pond's construction, also provide habitat for deer, especially in the wintertime. Tracks in the snow show that deer do come down to the entering tile water opening in the ice, although not too frequently. I suspect that deer in this area rarely get hard up for either food or water. With all the alfalfa, winter wheat fields and waste grain, it would be like starving in the middle of a grocery store.

During the deer hunting season, our sons and their friends bag two or three deer (Figure 48) within a quarter mile of the pond every year. The deer population in our county has increased dramatically over the past twenty-five years, as witness the fact that we hadn't seen a whitetail at all, until one was killed by an auto in front of our house in 1962. Now we see deer as an almost weekly occurrence and deer-auto collisions are a common source of insurance claims in McHenry County.

Forty-six acres of wildlife habitat in the form of woodlot (21 acres), pine tree plantation (five acres), grass waterway (three acres) and conservation reserve plants (17 acres), provides convenient cover close to the pond for many species of birds and mammals. Although we do see much evidence of some of these animals, I must admit disappointment in not observing more evidence of rabbits and pheasants in the past ten years. Why they seem to be low in number, I don't know. I guess I'll have to talk with a wildlife biologist again and get his or her opinion. The DNR Private Lands Biologist has set me up with a wildlife habitat improvement plan just recently, and I'll begin the first phase of the plan this spring.

Waterfowl

One of the add-on benefits to having your own pond is that you will be visited by ducks and geese and other birds that like the water or wetland environment (Figure W.). I didn't give a whole lot of thought or planning to this aspect when I had the pond constructed, but as it turns out, I fell into providing a good habitat for several species of birds, the dabbling or "puddle" ducks in particular. That came about when a large portion (2/3) of the water in our two acre pond ended up being less than five feet deep and also by the surrounding woodlands with a lot of oak trees and corn, wheat and soybean farm fields being nearby.

The shallow water area encouraged the growth of submerged pondweeds, which most waterfowl like to feed upon, likewise emergent wetland plants, like smartweed, bullrushes and cattails, which provide both food and shelter. The oak trees are seasonally loaded with acorns, a very important part of the diet of wood ducks and to some extent mallards. The field crops of soybeans,

Figure W. Sightings of birds associated with water, or on the pond, between 1967 and 1996*.

Species	Jan.	Feb.	Mar.	Apr.	May	June	July	Aug.	Sept.	Oct.	Nov.
Bluewing teal				6	117	36	15		363	207	13
Wood duck			56	110	80	56	103	41	21	29	2
Mallard			130	98	33	4	30	9	12	70	10
Canada goose		4	112	81	17		53	40	44	41	30
North. shovelor	2	24									
Amer. Widgeon	7	6									
Black duck										7	
Ringneck duck				11							
Goldeneye				6							
Bufflehead				1							5
Whistling swan											1
Lesser scaup			14		20						2
American coot					12	13			1	12	
Common merganser			1	6		4			1		
Piedbill grebe					1			2	10	6	2
Great blue heron		2	6		4	11	10	12	13	2	
Green heron					4	16	9	9	15	5	
Bl. crown night heron							5				
Sandhill crane**			126	7							204
American bittern			1								
Kingfisher				2					2	5	2

* no birds seen in December
** flying over only

wheat and corn also provide a food source to ducks and geese when unharvested or waste grain lies about on the ground. Geese are frequently seen in large numbers in our winter wheat fields shortly after the seeds germinate and wheat emerges in September, because the Canada goose is a notorious grazer and loves to pull up newly emerged grasses.

One shouldn't overlook the fact that if fish, frogs and crayfish are in a pond, one may be assured to get visits from the fish-eating birds, like great blue herons, green herons, night herons, kingfishers, grebes, mergansers, and cormorants. These birds, and even some ducks, enjoy foraging on aquatic critters and also include aquatic insects in their diet.

The observations I made of water birds in the initial years of the pond were rather casual. By 1983, I began taking better notes of the birds I saw and at least some of the time using a camera and binoculars. This aided in identifying birds through the use of various texts, like *Ducks, Geese and Swans of North America,* by Bellrose (1980), and helped to confirm identification and habits. Some waterfowl, such as teal and wood ducks, took me awhile to sort out until I learned the different sounds they make and their flight and flocking behavior. Immature ducks and hens also give me trouble because of their neutral coloration. Forgiving these limitations, let me recount some interesting facts I have learned.

The dabbling, or "puddle" duck species are the most abundant visitors to our pond. Although I have identified 14 different species of waterfowl (Figure W), there are four which really dominate the numbers. In order, they are: bluewing teal, wood ducks, mallards and Canada geese. Although the bluewing teal has been more abundant numerically, I have actually made more daily sightings of wood ducks. This is because the teal are often present in large numbers of 15 to 50, while woodies are usually seen one or two pairs at a time. Also, wood ducks, because they nest near the pond, are present persistently from March through August, while teal are bunched up in April-May and in August-September, representing their spring and fall migrations. Likewise, mallards appear mostly during their migration months in the spring and fall. Oddly, I have never identified a pintail duck on or near our pond.

I have not encouraged duck hunting on our pond, other than by my own sons and an occasional friend. In thirty years, less than twenty ducks and only two Canada geese have been taken, to my knowledge.

Species by Species Discussion

Wood duck

Following a number of years of seeing wood ducks using the pond, we decided to put up some wood duck nesting boxes. In 1978, the first box was placed in an oak tree, about twenty feet up its trunk. The tree was located fifty feet from the pond's edge. The box was constructed of wood following a design found in a Illinois Department of Conservation magazine. Two years later, my son and his friend put up two additional wood duck nesting boxes using the same design. These, however, were mounted on poles driven into the pond bottom in shallow water (Figure 50). One was about 3-1/2 feet above the surface, at normal water level, and the other six feet off the water. The first was mounted on an iron pipe and the second on a square, wooden pole. I placed fine sawdust in the bottom of the boxes each spring. Although other birds have also used these boxes, I believe that all of them have been used by wood ducks for nesting at one time or another. I could see into only the lower box easily, while standing in my canoe, but needed to use a ladder to see into the higher boxes.

The original wooden box we put up in the oak tree fell apart after eleven years. The other two were still useable after being up for twelve years, although I have had to make occasional repairs. These boxes have been used for nesting as recently as the year 1994. Also in 1994, I put up a plastic, cylindrical wood duck box which is distributed by Ducks Unlimited. This one I attached to a post about ten feet high on the peninsula which juts into the pond (Figure 51). It was used by some bird other than a wood duck for nesting soon after I put it up.

The first brood of newly hatched wood ducklings I observed was on June 30, 1977, a year before we put up the initial artificial nesting box. There are a number of oak trees in the woods which have natural cavities, so I suspect the woodies used one of these for a nesting spot. I have seen the drakes (Figure 52) and hens in late April, exploring cavities in trees as far away (800 feet) from the pond as our house, even though the nesting boxes were available. Most young ducklings have been observed in late May, June and July. Because incubation takes about 30 days, one could assume egg laying is occurring from April to perhaps late June. Hens with as few as three and as many as fourteen ducklings have been sighted, always on the water. I have not observed a young duckling on land as of yet.

Eggs have been seen in the wood duck boxes in several different years, most frequently in early May. Always the eggs were similar in description to wood ducks eggs described in the literature, i.e. about half the size of a chicken egg and almost white. However, I once encountered a much larger, white egg in a nesting box, which the wood duck hen later apparently dumped out of the box and into the pond, where I found it. I don't know what kind of bird was poaching, like a cowbird, on the wood duck's good graces, but it didn't work. I also once observed a little screech owl peering at me out of the entrance of a box. Maybe she laid the odd-ball egg I saw.

In 1993, the low wood duck box over the pond was apparently used as a "dump" nest. A dump nest is said to be one in which a number of hens may lay eggs, but do not incubate them. In August, I threw 23 rotten eggs out from this box. No wood duck was seen to use the box after May 19th. The tall box in the pond was also used for nesting, as I did see a hen present in May, but I don't know if any young were ever hatched out. When hens were actively using a box for nesting, there would always be fine, downy feathers present, mixed up with the sawdust I had placed in the box. I once observed little ducklings bailing out of their nest in the town of Havana, Illinois. When they hit the hard earth, they bounced about a foot off the ground, much like pingpong balls, got up and merrily followed the mother hen away to the nearby Illinois River, none the worse for wear. When young wood ducks are present at the pond and before they can fly, they will hide among the cattails whenever the adults are scared away.

In the winter of 1993-94, both wood duck boxes in the pond either fell apart or were pushed over by the ice. Henceforth, I have gone only with the plastic wood duck box on the peninsula. When I opened it up to clean it out the other day, February 16th, I found a little eastern screech owl staring back at me. It was sitting in a nest lined exclusively with red cardinal feathers (Figure 53).

Bluewing teal

I have counted a total of 749 bluewing teal using the pond since 1967. Sometimes when they and the wood ducks are using the pond at the same time, I have had trouble differentiating between them at a distance, because they're both small . However, once they flush off the water, the wood duck hen gives a characteristic "squeal" which cannot be mistaken. Bluewing teal also tend to "sit" a little lower in the water than do wood ducks.

Teal have rarely nested around my pond. Only once have I observed a hen with a brood of teal ducklings and this numbered fourteen little ones, occurring on June 8, 1978.

Spring sightings of teal on the pond were usually in pairs in April and May. Very few have been seen again until August and September (Figure W), when large flocks of fifty may be present at a given time. A few have used the pond in October and none after that month, leading me to conclude that they must be one of the earliest species in their southward fall migration. This has resulted in the fact that only a few teal have been shot off the pond in the fall duck hunting season in thirty years.

Mallards

Although I have seen large flocks of mallards flying over the farm in V-formation, the most I have observed on the pond at one time is fifteen. In the spring they are usually present in March and April in pairs and are frequently the very first duck observed as the ice is going out. Mallards are also one of the latest to be seen, with sightings up to the end of November. Some hardy individuals apparently wait for the new, complete ice cover to force them to fly to southward climes.

Mallards are easy for me to identify for four reasons: 1. The adult greenheaded drake can hardly be mistaken, 2. They are considerably larger than other puddle ducks, 3. They allow the observer to get reasonably close before they "spook" off the pond, and 4. They are sometimes very noisy with loud, conversational quacking, reminding me a little of my wife's bridge club.

Waterfowl and aeration

I began operating an aerator system, off and on, in the pond since the fall of 1978. It appears to me that both ducks and geese are somewhat more reluctant to land on the pond while the aerator is running. Perhaps the bubbles or turbulence makes them more wary. There have been times when ducks *were* present with the aerator running, however they did not seem to approach the area of turbulence very closely.

Canada geese

Fourth in abundance on the pond has been the Canada goose. Although I first saw geese on one of our fields in the fall of 1975, it was not until September of 1979, that I saw the first goose actually on the pond water and then not again until April of 1982, which was eighteen years after it was first constructed. Since then, we have seen Canada geese using the pond more and more frequently with each passing year.

I haven't seen a brood of young goslings on the pond yet, however I know that they nest successfully at a golf course a mile away. The increase in local nesting may account for the building numbers of geese we see, especially during the summer. Another attraction to geese is the waste grain present in the farm fields in the fall and also the winter wheat which may be germinating in September and present through the next May. I saw flocks of geese several times grazing on our newly emerged winter wheat in late September of 1993 and April of 1994. Oddly, we have not yet seen a goose on the pond in the month of June. Perhaps this corresponds to a time when they are caring for their young goslings somewhere else and are somewhat confined to near their nesting territory.

Lament of the Canada Goose

So, what's the matter down there on the ground?
Grey and green gunk falling from the sky
On your aluminum siding, sidewalks and Buicks?
It makes me want to cry.

We've been flying up here for untold millennia
and no one's complained until now
that you humans have littered the earth with targets
which we can hardly miss.

Our cloaca's open twenty times a day
walking, sitting or flying
and with that many objects on the ground
I don't think the airlines are lying

When they blame it on us.

Author

Canada geese do not seem to be very shy and will frequently land on the pond even though I am nearby. Consequently, I have been able to get some good photos of them, while at the same time being impressed by the nearness of these large birds. A nostalgic reminder of spring's arrival is hearing the honking of geese headed north in formation over our farm.

Geese, wood ducks and mallards seem somewhat tolerant of each other, even on my relatively small pond. They are often present in combination at the same time. The most frequent sightings of geese occur in March and April (Figure W). We see lesser numbers of geese in May, July and October and have yet to see a Canada goose on the pond after November 15th. Only two geese have been shot off the pond and none anywhere else on the farm, even though their presence can be a little frustrating a times. Besides the pulling up of the winter wheat, geese can create a mess wherever they lounge in large numbers. I counted 67 fresh, fecal droppings in the grass on the dam after a day of their "socializing" there. According to the literature, geese defecate almost hourly and can impact on water quality if they remain on a small lake or pond for very long. Their droppings contain about 5% nitrogen and 1-1/2% phosphorus (dry weight). The largest number of geese I have seen on the pond itself was more than 100 individuals on October 18, 1986.

Sightings of ten other species of waterfowl on the pond between 1983 and 1996 are also included in Figure W. Why some of these species stopped over at the pond when they normally prefer somewhat different habitats, like large lakes or marshes (shoveler, wigeon), I do not know. Maybe some individuals get lost during migration, or others may be crippled. The latter was true of the only whistling (tundra) swan, a bird which forced me to look frantically through three waterfowl identification books. Its usual fall migration corridor is more than a hundred miles north of our pond's location.

On April 15, 1975, I could hear ducks on the pond from all the way up at our house. I decided to sneak down to the pond from behind the dam. When I did this, very carefully, and peeked over the top of the dam I could see ducks of every description paddling in groups by species. I dared not raise up any further, but peeking through the grass I could see at least eight species, some which were quite unusual—like the ringneck and northern shovelor. There were so many ducks that I couldn't count them. I suppose the presence of some migrating ducks at this time had simply decoyed more and more until the pond was nearly full. I have never seen such a conglomeration since and this one will stick vividly in my memory.

Shorebirds and other water-loving birds

Conspicuous because of their large size have been the great blue herons visiting the pond for many years. Its slow, halting walk around shallow water, looking for fish, frogs and other water animals cannot be mistaken, neither can its measured, broad wingbeat and curved neck in flight. Although they rarely appear more than two at a time, I have seen these herons in every month from March through November, with the exception of May. We see them most frequently from July through October. I have also seen great blues at the pond with large fish in their bills. Some of the fish which I know were killed by great blue heron include a one pound largemouth bass, a twenty-two inch northern pike and a one pound channel catfish. With such appetites they must eat great numbers of smaller fish.

The green heron is almost as frequent a visitor as the great blue. I did see five of these shorebirds at one time in August. I suspect the feeding habits of these two heron species are similar. The occasional appearance of a dead or injured fish in the water

Figure G . Great blue heron.

with a hole drilled in its head or back (Figure 54), strongly hints that a heron or maybe a kingfisher muffed one of its opportunities. The green heron is only half the size of the great blue. I have seen neither species nesting near the pond. I also am guilty of occasionally mixing up the green heron with the black-crowned night heron if I don't get close enough. Granting a few lapses on my part, sightings of black-crown night herons have been infrequent.

And speaking of kingfishers, if anyone is, I see the belted kingfisher off and on throughout the open water season. Looking like an oversize bluejay with a crest, they like to fly low and swiftly with deep wing beats over the pond's surface, or perch up in a tree nearby with a good view of the pond. It sometimes makes a loud, rattling call and can dive headfirst, like a kamikaze, into the water after its prey.

About the only way I can figure to get good camera shots of some of the more evasive birds is to build a blind, similar to a duck blind, close to the water's edge and just wait there until the opportunity arises. So far, I haven't gotten the ambition to do this, but maybe some day . . . I am also going to need to invest in a better, long-range lens attachment for my 35 mm camera. I have been using a f 28 - 200 mm telephoto lens, but find it to be inadequate at times for long distances. Taking pictures off hand of moving or flying birds is not easy, especially under varying light conditions. I've got a lot of blurred photos to prove this, but fortunately I have a few good ones which keep me going. I have a camera with me about 20% of the time when I go down to the pond. The other 80% of the time is when I see things that are interesting to photograph. Why are birds in easy camera range only when I don't have my camera with me? More likely it is my lack of patience which leads to lack of good pictures.

Another large and interesting bird that we have seen flying over, although never landing on the pond, is the sandhill crane. We see them either flying north in March, or south in November. Their time-table is very specific. I first will hear their loud, chirping or chortling sound, like young chickens in conversation and then I can look up and see flocks of from five to fifty birds high up in the air and frequently going around in circles. I have only begun to see them in the past seven or eight years and I suspect their warm weather base may be up in Wisconsin, likely at the Horicon Marsh Wildlife Refuge.

Among the other birds commonly seen around the pond is the redwing blackbird (Figure 55). They are present in numbers from mid-March through October and like to roost and nest among the cattails which surround the pond. Their small eggs are blue with brown flecks (Figure 56) and hatch in the first part of July. They must also be among the most demonstrative of birds, with their loud, chattering scolding of anyone approaching, along with their habit of conspicuously displaying their red shoulder patches during warmer weather.

Another frequent bird around the pond is the swallow. I know the barn swallow is present, because I can identify its deeply forked tail and the brightly colored adult male. However, there are likely one or more other species of swallow also using the pond. They fly frequently and swiftly over the surface, dipping lightly into the water. I presume they are picking up insects off the surface when they do this. Almost always, there are several birds present at one time and I see them perching, like posing beauty queens, on electric lines near my house. They make mud nests in the rafters of our barn and the dog sometimes catches one while they are flying up against the inside of the barn windows.

When the pond level is low in dry, warm weather, exposing areas of mud flats, we see numbers of spotted sandpipers walking on the wet mud with their tails bobbing up and down. Because there are often snails exposed on the mud, I would guess they are feeding upon them, however aquatic insects and plant seeds may also be present to entice the birds. We rarely see the sandpipers unless the pond is low. Other species of sandpipers and plovers, which I cannot identify, may also be present, because I see a discrepancy in the sizes of these birds. Lately, I have been seeing the yellow legs, a marsh sandpiper. It also walks the mud flats when the pond is low. I know the killdeer has visited us now and then, also under low water conditions and I once saw an American bittern, trying to disguise itself as a weed, standing with its beak pointed straight up to zenith. This is a bird species which is classified as "endangered" in Illinois.

A great many of these shorebird and sandpiper species spend their summers far to the north, often in the Canadian tundra. Once in a great while we see some herring gulls. They will come this far inland from Lake Michigan, particularly if the weather is quite bad on the big lake for several days in a row. More often they are seen on nearby garbage landfills, a seemingly unlikely surrounding for a bird which is dressed in nearly pure white feathers, like a pristine nurse's uniform.

Fish

The greatest single incentive for me to have a pond of my own was my interest in fish and fishing. When I was nine years old, I would walk down to the much-polluted Des Plaines River and try to catch bullheads on garden worms, a string and a number six hook. When we would swim in the river, we would use a stroke we named, "The Des Plaines River Crawl". This consisted of pushing the surface debris out of the way as we swam forward. By the time I was 14, I would ride my bicycle, during summer vacation, the 20 miles up to Lake Zurich or Diamond Lake, and either fish from the shoreline, or pool my financial resources with a friend, and rent a row boat at a resort. On a good day, we might come back with a stringer of bluegills dangling from our handlebars. Mind you, this was before World War II. A child wouldn't dare brave the traffic with a bike today. Later, when I went to college under the G.I. Bill, I majored in aquatic biology and specialized in fisheries. Why wouldn't I want a pond? Add to this the fact that I consider the pan-fried filet of bass or bluegill, dipped in egg batter and cornflake crumbs, to be amongst the finest eating that exists on this globe.

The fish management aim in ponds in Illinois is usually to maintain largemouth bass and bluegills in combination. The reason is simple. In our warm, fertile waters, these two species form a natural chain or balance within their water environment. The bluegills feed mostly upon aquatic insects, and the bass feed upon larger aquatic animals, such as crayfish and frogs and also upon bluegills and young bass. This rationale may seem too simple, but it works time and again.

Perhaps the only living organism which a bass may prefer to eat over a small bluegill, is a crayfish or "crawdad" (Figure 57). For that matter, almost every creature that hangs around a pond, whether it be bass, heron, duck, raccoon or mink, considers the small crayfish to be the "piece de resistance".

Stocking year

In 1966, we stocked both largemouth bass and bluegills soon after the pond had been filled with water for two years. Introduced were 150 young-of-the-year bass, averaging one inch in length and 100 young-of-the-year bluegills, averaging two inches. I have also experimented with stocking several other species of fish, which will be discussed later, but this initial bass and bluegill stocking has formed the basis of the pond's fish population for the many years up to and including the present (Figure F).

Growth of these newly-introduced fish (Figure 58) was very fast. Within six weeks I already could see bluegills, now almost four inches in length, making their saucer-shaped spawning nests in shallow water. These bluegills spawned successfully, as we were able to capture numerous very tiny bluegills in a net in mid-September that same year. This is somewhat akin, heaven forbid, to humans having babies when they're eleven years old. Ordinarily, bluegills are expected to be at least a year of age before they are sexually mature. Also collected in the net were a few of the stocked bass which were already nearly six inches long at four months of age.

Stocking plus one year

Rapid growth like this is not unusual in a new pond, as there is a lot of food to go around for the relatively few fish that are introduced. The next spring after stocking, I caught more bass and bluegills in a seine to observe. The bass which had been stocked were still averaging about six inches (Figure 59), and the original bluegills were now four to six inches. The bluegills which

Figure F. Fish Species Time Line of Presence

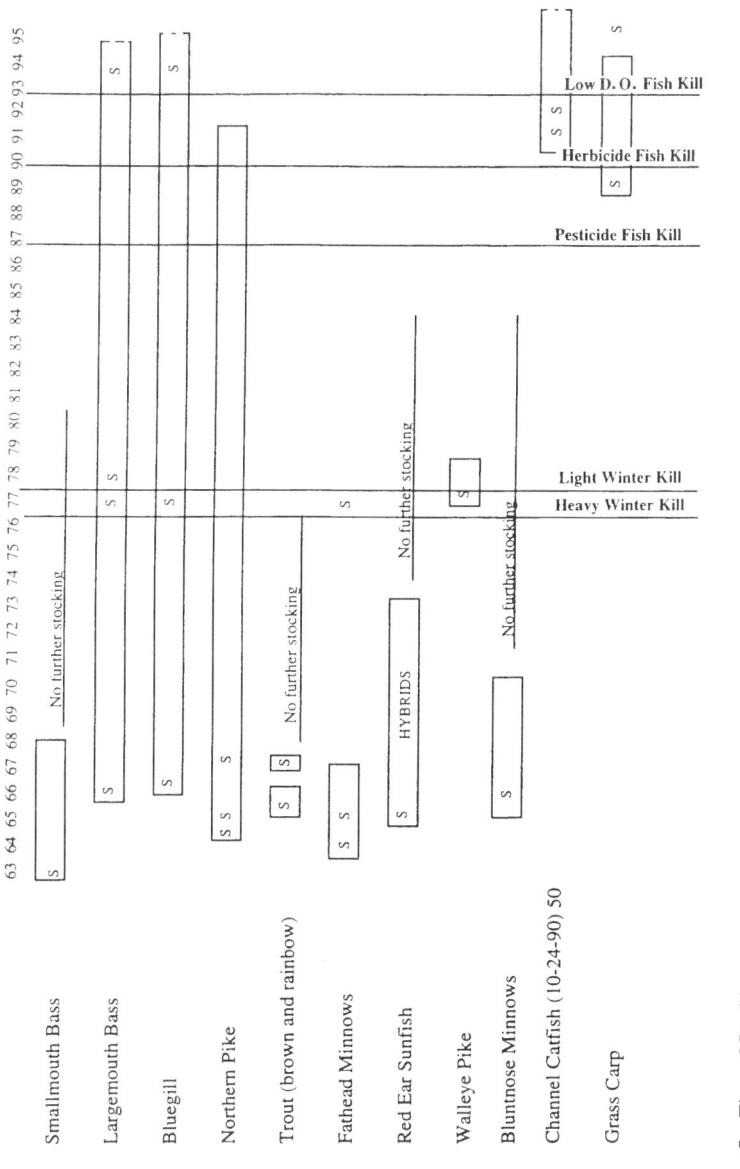

had hatched out in the pond the previous year, now averaged 1-1/2 inches, and were numerous. In an attempt to prevent the bluegills from becoming too abundant, I threw out all the small ones I would catch in the net. Adult bluegills again formed spawning nests in June and six-inch bass were readily visible everywhere. A few of the cannibalistic (they eat each other) bass were now nine inches long. The original bluegill stocking of the previous year had grown from two inches, to where they averaged 5-1/2 inches in length. By August, an abundance of young-of the-year bluegill could be taken in a net. I took as many as a thousand out of the pond at one time.

By late September, 15 months after stocking, we were able to catch bass readily which now averaged over nine inches, on black, plastic worms. We returned the bass to the water, but would still throw out all the small bluegills we would catch, either on hook and line or in a seine. The fact that we saw no very small bass this second year demonstrated that bass reproduction had not yet taken place.

Stocking plus two years

July of the following year, two years after their introduction, we could see schools of small (one-inch) bass, which by late August had grown to two inches. Bass reproduction had been successful. By wintertime, bluegills were being caught readily through the ice, along with an occasional bass. The objective in our throwing all the bass we caught back into the pond the first two years, was to make certain there were ample numbers present for their first spawning period.

Stocking plus three years

In July, three years after the little bass and bluegills were first stocked, a second spawn of bass was observed, with schools of half-inch bass here and there during the first week of July. The bass which were hatched out the previous year were now three to four inches in length, and the original bass were now twelve inches long and about a pound in weight. The bluegills had spawned every year since they were stocked and by 1969, it was getting difficult to differentiate between the earlier year classes, with sizes now beginning to overlap (Figure Y).

Figure Y. Largemouth bass and bluegill growth for initial four years after stocking (1966-1969).

	1966	
	July size	Comment
1966 Largemouth bass	1"	Initial stocking of 150 yoy*
1966 Bluegill	2"	Initial stocking of 100 yoy
	1967	
1966 Largemouth bass	6-9"	Yearlings
1966 Bluegill	5-1/2"	Yearlings + 1st yr. reprod.
1967 Bluegill	1"	Current year reprod.
	1968	
1966 Largemouth bass	9-10"	Two years old
1968 Largemouth bass	1"	Current year reprod.
1966 Bluegill	7-1/2"	Original stocking
1966 Bluegill	4-1/2"	1966 reprod.
1967 Bluegill	1-1/2"	One year old
1968 Bluegill	1/2"	Current year reprod.
	1969	
1966 Largemouth bass	13-14"	Original stock, now 3 yrs old
1968 Largemouth bass	3-4"	Yearlings
1969 Largemouth bass	1/2"	Young of the year
1966 Bluegill		Sizes now overlapping
1966 Bluegill	5-8"	among all three groups
1967 Bluegill		
1968 Bluegill	4"	Yearlings
1969 Bluegill	2"	Young of year in Sept.

* yoy = young of the current year

The pond almost winterkilled the winter of 1969-'70 because there was a lot of snow on the ice. Dissolved oxygen in the water got critically low; however, when the ice went off only a couple of dead fish showed up. That spring we were able to catch a number of highly-colored male bluegills off their spawning nests. It is the male that makes the spawning nest and stands guard over the eggs—the same as for bass. Males also "baby sit" their young, newly hatched offspring while they are still in schools, protecting them from predators, up until they are about six weeks of age.

Stocking plus four years

In the summer, four years after they were first introduced, we were catching bass from 7 to 13 inches in length. That fall, bass as large as 16 inches were caught. Both bass and bluegills brought off successful spawns again this year. We began keeping some of the bass and most of the bluegills that we caught on hook and line, which were large enough for eating purposes.

The value of managing the fishery for largemouth bass and bluegills in my pond has been strongly reinforced through thirty years. They demonstrate their adaptability to small ponds and lakes through the fact that they grow well, reproduce, and provide a lot of fishing opportunity, both in the warm weather and through the ice.

Over the years, I have continued to encourage fishermen to take out any bluegill they would catch, regardless of size. I also removed bluegills that were caught with my sampling devices (seines, traps, etc.) Sometimes I would destroy bluegill spawning nests (Figure 60) with a rake, to discourage reproduction. They are easy to distinguish from bass spawning nests, although their shape and size is quite similar, in that bluegills will almost always nest in colonies of from ten to twenty nests in close proximity. Bass spawning nests will be spaced a substantial distance apart.

Recreational fishing

After the pond was 12 years old, I began restricting fishermen to taking only one bass that they might catch in a day. At this time there was evidence that bluegills were becoming more dominant with each passing year and I wanted to bolster the bass population through offering them added protection. If I could maintain a strong bass population, they would provide better control of bluegills through predation than I could by trying to remove bluegills myself. As one might guess, many fishermen wanted to fish only for bass and not bluegills, but restricting them to one bass per day seemed to work fairly well in maintaining a healthy balance between the two species. How many fishermen might "cheat" on this arbitrary catch limit, I do not know, but I think most of them were quite scrupulous.

The largest bass that has been caught so far, was six pounds and strangely enough, by an antique collector in the little nearby town of Union. Some bluegills as large as nine inches (Figure 61) have been caught. Bluegill fishing is occasionally quite good through the ice, but bass are not often caught in the winter. I have noticed that fish do not seem to be as active when I run my aerator, particularly in the winter. This may be because the deeper water temperature is slightly *lower* under aeration conditions, with some open water, than it is when the ice completely covers the pond.

Sometimes people would fish the pond without permission. It is difficult for them to do this when we are at home, because it is almost necessary to pass the house on the way to the pond. I think it happened most frequently when we would be on vacation. We are more concerned about this in the wintertime, because of the hazard of someone falling through the ice. I am aware of only a couple of times in thirty years that a hunter has poached waterfowl off the pond.

Most fishermen are selective about what they want to catch and/or keep. For my pond, the order of preference was: 1. Bass; 2. Northern pike; 3. Bluegills. For the health of the pond, I would have preferred, of course, that their ranking of preference be reversed and I tried hard to convince fishermen of this.

The largemouth bass and bluegill are only two of the eleven different species of fish I have stocked in the pond since 1963. Of eleven different species I have introduced (Figure F), only five have maintained themselves more than six years. Three species have made the grade more than 20 consecutive years, i.e., largemouth bass, bluegills and northern pike.

The only access fish have to the pond is through stocking. There are no ponds or streams in the upper watershed to the pond, whereby escaped fish might find access. Because the spillway pipe is a five foot vertical drop, there is also no access to the pond from below; i.e. fish cannot swim *upstream* into the pond in times of heavy overflow or flooding. No kind of fish, other than what we have stocked, have appeared in the pond during its 32-year lifespan with one exception.

Following the fish die-off of 1994, I caught several bass and bluegills from a friend's pond about four miles away and transported them live to our pond. My son and grandson decided to be helpful and transported some bluegills they had caught from another pond nearby, and stocked them into ours. I suspect that amongst these "bluegills" were a few green sunfish, or perhaps green sunfish X bluegill hybrids. The latter are not easy to distinguish from a pure bluegill, and one needs to look carefully to tell the difference. Even if only a few hybrid green sunfish X bluegill were stocked, there is a certain percentage of fertility in these hybrids, and they can produce a few viable young if reproducing with a bluegill. In any event *now* (fall of '95), I have a substantial portion of my panfish population consisting of hybrid green sunfish X bluegills, along with some young largemouth bass.

The moral to this story is, if you don't want any undesirable species of fish introduced into your pond, make sure you have *total control* over any fish brought into your pond or lake. Even commercial fish dealers can have the wrong species mixed up with the right ones they deliver to you. I have observed this more than once not only with bluegills, but also with tiny yellow perch mixed up with tiny walleye pike.

How does one get fish for stocking?

Besides corresponding with your State Department of Natural Resources (DNR), usually the Fish Division, one may also be able to get the common fish species for stocking from the local county's Soil and Water Conservation District. These would include fish like bass and bluegills, channel catfish and white amur (grass carp). The State DNR may refer a person to any number of commercial sources for purchasing fish, if the state

DNR cannot, indeed, provide fish itself. Most states require fish dealers to be specially licensed.

Fish sampling

One way I find out about what's going on with the fish population, is simply by knowing what people are catching. When I look at these fish and open up their stomachs, I can also tell something about what they're eating and any diseases they may have.

There are also a number of other ways we have sampled the fish population through the years: seines of various lengths and meshes of several sizes, different kinds of fish traps (Figure 62), gill nets of several lengths and meshes, electrofishing from a boat, and once I even used the chemical "rotenone" to kill off fish in a very small area. Different kinds of sampling devices are adept at catching certain fish and not others. The small mesh seines are good for sampling young bass and bluegills. The gill nets are good for sampling northern pike and channel catfish in weedy areas. Electrofishing is good at catching adult bass. Traps are better than seines also in sampling weedy areas.

If a fishery biologist wants to do a comprehensive job of fish sampling on a given body of water, he or she usually uses several different sampling devices, although using the device may present a hazard. Once when I was sampling with a shocker from a boat, I fell into the water between the electrodes. Thus, I was able to live the catatonic experience, first hand, that a large fish might go through when shocked with electricity. Fortunately for me I survived, once I was properly weighed and measured by my partner after he picked me out of the water.

A word of caution: Some states may require scientific collection permits in order to collect fish with certain devices, even in your own pond. It is best to check with your state's Department of Natural Resources to find out what is legal and what is not.

Access to the water with a boat was simplified by making a boat launching ramp of sorts next to the beach. My son Kevin, who was working with construction at the time, provided me with a number of concrete planks, each 14 inches wide by four feet long, and steel bar reinforced. We placed these on the pond bottom, extending out from shore about twelve feet. I could back my boat trailer out on this ramp and far enough into the water to be able to float it off the trailer, if the pond level were up to normal. It wasn't difficult to place these planks into the water with two people lifting, and they're still there fifteen years later, albeit covered with a little mud.

Early spring fish observations

While I'm discussing methods of observing the fish population in the pond, I want to be sure to mention a seasonal peculiarity we have noted. In the early spring, for about three or four weeks after the ice goes out and the water temperature is still less than 44°F, the pond appears for all purposes to be devoid of fish. Walking around the perimeter of the pond, or canoeing in the pond may not reveal a single fish, even though the water may be very clear. One might not be able to catch a fish on hook and line in this cold water period, and may jump to the conclusion that the fish have disappeared over the winter. Quite simply, fish like bass and bluegills are *not* very active in these cold water temperatures, and may be lying under whatever cover is present in the water, algae or dead cattails, and not showing themselves. Oddly enough, bass and bluegills may be more active under the ice cover when they may be caught ice fishing, than in that immediate period after the ice leaves. On the other hand, if one has northern pike or trout in a body of water, they may be active and visible as soon as the ice leaves.

In any event, over the years I have learned to be patient about looking for fish in the early spring. I don't panic unless I see dead fish floating around when the ice goes out.

Fish diseases

For me to say, "Fish have diseases!", is about as astounding as my saying, "I had pimples when I was a kid". Fish are subject to many kinds of diseases in most water environments. In the following pages I'm going to allude to those which have been especially debilitating to fish in our pond, or especially conspicuous.

Bass in the pond, both largemouth and smallmouth, have sometimes been infected with tapeworms. This was especially the case just four years after we first stocked them. At this time almost all of the larger bass had tapeworms in their intestines and were becoming thin. The cycle of the tapeworm is such that it is found in a small water animal, which is in turn eaten by a small fish, like a bluegill, where it becomes encysted. When the bluegill is eaten by a bass, the tapeworm becomes an adult and is quite visible in the fish's gut. The eggs from this adult tapeworm pass out of the bass through its feces and are picked up by other small water animals, thus completing the cycle. Bass with heavy tapeworm infections, besides becoming thin, may also become sterile. The tapeworm cannot be passed on to a human by eating the cooked fish.

Largemouth bass

I want to say some special things about bass that I haven't already discussed. In the spring I first see bass spawning nests being made in mid-May. Frequently, the first nests I see have been made along the dam in two to four feet of water depth. Unlike bluegills, bass nests are never any closer to each other than perhaps fifteen feet. Apparently papa bass, who makes the nest and takes care of the eggs, cannot tolerate another nesting bass too nearby. I have not seen a bass on the spawning nest less than about eleven inches in length.

Anywhere from June through July, I am likely to see newly hatched bass swimming in schools parallel to the shoreline. Usually the male bass can also be seen nearby, protecting them. The number of little bass in these schools are great, probably around five to 10,000. I strongly suspect that these schools sometimes join up with each other, as I have seen numbers of these very young bass that seem enormous. When they get to be a certain size, they split out of their schools and go their own way. I think maybe this occurs when they get big enough to eat each other. This happens when they get an inch and a half, or larger.

Young bass and bluegills, particularly those less than four inches in length, seem susceptible to being washed over the spillway and out of the pond, during periods of heavy rainfall and overflow. I noted this particularly on June 17th of 1980, when I saw starlings picking the fish out of the grass below the dam. I have seen it at other times also.

Bluegills

Bluegills make their spawning nests as much as a month later than bass, maybe even as late as July. The male bluegills like to make their nests in colonies very close to one another. There may be anywhere from five to thirty nests in a colony, in twelve to 22 inches of water. Each nest may run as large as 18 inches in diameter and four inches in depth. They are not as large as bass nests. From year to year, bluegills may not locate their nests in the same area, but are almost always in the same depth of water, and shallower than the bass nests. I have seen male bluegills as small as four inches on a spawning nest.

Very young bluegills in small schools may be seen after hatching, but not as often as young bass. It may be that the bluegills break out of their schools sooner than do bass. When in schools, they must be very susceptible to predation. When they break out of their schools, they quickly head for vegetative cover, the same as the little bass. They are running for their lives. That is why, when I do any fish sampling in the summer, and I bring up a wad of aquatic plants, small bluegills and bass frequently fall out of them. They'll even hide in filamentous algae.

Sometimes a yellow grub is found in the flesh of a bluegill caught from the pond. This is the fluke, Clinostomum, the adult stage of which is a parasite in a fish-eating bird, like a heron.

The Future

The fish population and the fishing in the pond has certainly had its ups and downs over the past thirty years. I think it's safe to say that we will rely upon largemouth bass and bluegills to continue to provide the main fishing in the future, although I may try to introduce northern pike again.

As far as the present fish are concerned, with the young,

hybrid bluegill X green sunfish being in the pond, I'm going to give them a year to see how they get along with the young largemouth bass. If it looks like the green sunfish are going to overwhelm the bass, I will have no hesitancy to eliminate all the fish chemically and start over again. This is done by introducing the organic chemical rotenone (5%) at a dosage of 4 mg/L, probably either in the month of May or September. Rotenone has been used for many years for this purpose and is safe to use, both due to its low toxicity to humans and other warm-blooded animals and because it breaks down rapidly in the presence of sunlight and warm water. But then, nature may eliminate all the fish through winterkill and save me all the trouble messing around with chemicals. The present winter (1996-97) looks like a bad one, with opaque ice and persistent snow cover.

If a pond or lake owner wishes to undertake this chemical procedure, which fishery biologists tactfully call, "fish rehabilitation", one must first contact their state's Department of Natural Resources. The use of rotenone for this purpose is restricted in most, if not all states.

Smallmouth bass

The first species of fish that I introduced into my new pond was the smallmouth bass. I was familiar with smallmouths mostly from stream work I had done in Illinois, and from sport fishing in northern lakes in Wisconsin. It is a fish whose game qualities I admire greatly, but I knew they did not survive well in ponds in Illinois, when in competition with other fishes, particularly sunfish. Therefore, I chose to stock only smallmouth bass in November of 1963, putting in 65 fish which were 3 inches in length, and were fish hatched out in that year.

The smallmouth is more of an insect feeder when young and can do alright without other fish to forage upon. I did later stock some fathead minnows for food, both in the fall of '64 and the spring of '65. Growth of these young smallmouths was beyond my fondest wishes. They grew to an average of 5-1/2 inches in length by the May following stocking and to 9-1/2 inches by that

September. I was hoping these fish would be mature in 1965, and that they would successfully spawn. If I had found that to occur, I would have considered devoting the pond only to smallmouth bass for several more years.

We fished for smallmouths mainly by spin fishing and fly casting and we didn't keep any smallmouths we caught for the first two years they were in the pond, although 9 to 13 inch bass were quite easy to catch by early 1965. In the spring of '65, I searched the shallow waters of the pond in vain for evidence of smallmouth spawning nests. I could find none until May 18th, when I observed nine smallmouth bass males on their spawning nests. These nests were spaced widely apart and were fanned down to coarse rock and gravel. About this same time, I had stocked 75 northern pike fry, about one inch long, from some eggs I had collected in the wild. I didn't hold much hope for these little pike to escape being eaten by the bass.

Four days after I first found the smallmouth nests, I could see newly hatched "swim-up" bass fry on four of the nests. They were nearly black in color at this time. Unfortunately, on June 13th, I treated the water with a chemical (Hydrathol 47) to kill fineleaf pondweed and chara which was appearing. Two days later, I could see very small, dead bass on the surface, but no dead adults. It seemed obvious that I had killed these little fish with the chemical I had used, as dissolved oxygen was still satisfactory in the water. By June and July, it was also apparent that I hadn't killed all the little smallmouths, as I could see the survivors which were now three inches in length.

One year later, May of 1966, these same bass which were now yearlings, were five inches long. Treatment of the plants in late May, with the same chemical I used the prior year, again killed a few of the bass. I could see some of the adult smallmouths, now three years old, on seven different spawning nests with eggs in late May; however by early June there were no fish on these nests, and I could see neither eggs nor young fish.

Because of my impatience to try other species of fish in the pond, I also stocked young bluegills and largemouth bass in July of 1966. This was the beginning of the end for the smallmouths.

Although the smallmouth continued to be present and even to spawn for the next three years, the numbers of their young dropped off significantly. Also, the body condition of the older smallmouths became thinner each year until 1968, when the last smallmouth that was caught was in an emaciated condition.

I attribute the "end" of the smallmouth mainly to my stocking of bluegills in 1966, and to the bluegills' rapid growth, reproduction and survival. The smallmouth cannot compete in northern Illinois ponds or lakes with the bluegill and largemouth bass. A fact which complicates this diagnosis, in our pond at least, is that the smallmouths became heavily infested with bass tapeworm, a debilitating intestinal parasite. The largemouth bass adults which were present in 1969, also were infected with this same parasite; however, they were capable of surviving.

The summary of my experience with the smallmouth bass in ponds or lakes in this part of the country is: If you want smallmouths, do *not* stock any other sunfish species—either bluegills or largemouth bass. You may end up with not as many fish to catch, using only smallmouths, but you'll have a lot of fun catching them. We did!

Northern Pike

I've always had a kind of "thing" about northern pike. Northern Illinois is about as far south as this species of fish is found. As a matter of fact, 40° latitude north is about the southern limit of the northern pike, whether you're in Russia, Sweden, or the USA. As a Department of Conservation biologist, I used to capture northern pike in the early spring, strip their eggs and fertilize them and then take these eggs to the Spring Grove Fish Hatchery, to be hatched and used for stocking.

It should come as no surprise to you, therefore, that I had to try northern pike in my pond. I had seen a few relatively small ponds, particularly in marshy areas, where northern pike were successful in maintaining themselves by natural reproduction. Apparently they were using these nearby areas of flooded vegetation in the spring as a place to lay their eggs. Other than laying and fertilizing the eggs in the proper place, northern pike parents do not give them any further attention. This makes them adult delinquents compared to bass and bluegills. As partial compensation for this parental neglect, the northern pike is capable of producing many times more eggs than sunfishes, sometimes upwards of 50,000 eggs.

I first stocked 75 northern pike fry (very young) in my pond in 1964, one year after it had been constructed. My interest at that time was in whether this species would survive at all, much less trying to build a population. Subsequent sampling of the pond with nets, during the remainder of that initial year, did not yield any evidence of these fish, so in May of 1965, I stocked 100 northern pike fry and 150 more in April of '67. I soon found out that the 1965-stocked fish had survived, as I caught two, which were already nine inches in length, in seine hauls at the end of July of '65.

By the time they were yearlings, these same northern pike had grown to an average of over 15 inches, and as two year olds (in 1967), were 21 inches long, and we were catching them readily on hook and line. Very rapid growth indeed, when one considers it usually requires northern pike three years to achieve this size. Because I considered it unlikely that pike would spawn successfully in my pond, I had stocked 150, which were about two inches in length in April of '67. By June of '68, these fish were about 17 inches in length and the original pike stocking were 26 inches at this time. We began allowing fishermen to keep any pike they caught over 20 inches in length by 1969.

Lo and behold, in 1972 I saw one little northern pike in the pond in July, that had to be a result of natural reproduction. I wasn't certain I was happy about this development, because by that time the pond was flourishing with a strong population of largemouth bass and bluegills. Bringing another very good predator fish onto the scene may very well upset the balance between bass and bluegills which had been achieved, but of course I could blame no one but myself.

After 1967, I did not do any further stocking of pike. In subsequent years I am certain that the pike brought off successful natural spawns in at least four additional years up to 1986. The last pike I saw was in 1991, when I netted an emaciated 20 incher. This means that the northerns maintained themselves in my pond from 1967 to 1991, entirely by natural reproduction.

Why and how did these fish manage to reproduce in a small, artificial pond off and on for over twenty years? I believe the secret is this: Certain years in the fall, the pond level would become quite low for an extended period of time. When this would happen for long enough, wetland plants like smartweed and sedges would grow out onto the exposed portion of the pond bottom. The following spring the pond would rise to full level and flood the remnants of these plants, and this is what the pike wanted to spawn their eggs upon in March and April. I was able to track this phenomenon in my pond observations, and it was always a sequence which was precursor to successful spawning and survival.

It was relatively easy to keep track of the northern pike because they were so readily caught by fishermen. Unlike many other fish species, they are also easily caught in the winter through the ice. My son, Kevin, likes to fish for northern pike through the ice, frequently using frozen smelt as bait. Also, I was able to catch pike easily in a gill net, and could usually return these fish to the pond alive, after I weighed and measured them. My sons also measured any pike they caught, whether they kept them to eat or threw them back.

Frequently, we made observations at night with a light around the pond's edge in early April. Unlike other fish species, the pike like to spawn at this early time of year. Sometimes we saw pike, sometimes we didn't. It became difficult to see into the water after 1976, because of the heavy cover that cattails were now providing in shallow water.

An important part of the make-up of northern pike should be mentioned here. This species can survive on relatively low dissolved oxygen conditions, which some other game fish species cannot. As a consequence it is somewhat resistant to winterkill. In two successive years of winterkill of fish on my pond, only two northern pike showed up dead. This was true even in the heavy fish kill of '77-'78. What this demonstrates is that the northern pike may have a place for introduction into shallow lakes which may be prone to winterkill, especially if they are in weedy or marshy environments.

Pike in my pond have at times been conspicuously vulnerable to one particular disease, black spot. This appears like large, pepper spots on the skin of the fish. It comes from a young fluke, *Neascus*, which as an adult is a parasite in a fish-eating bird, like the herons. Droppings from the heron into the pond water can introduce an immature form of this fluke which infects snails, and our pond has plenty of snails. Another later form of this fluke emerges from the snail and burrows into the fish's flesh, and hence becomes the black spot we see. There may be 50 or more spots on one fish. I have found lesser infections of black spot also on bass and bluegills.

To testify as to the predator ability of northern pike, I found a ten inch bass in the stomach of a 20 inch pike. I also found a 22 inch pike choked to death on a large bluegill, caught crosswise in its throat.

A funny thing happened about a northern pike that I caught in the pond. At the time, we had a family of Laotian people living with us, who had escaped from Laos to Cambodia and whom we sponsored as emigres to this country. I caught a three pound northern pike on my spinning rod, brought it up to the house and fileted it, pan frying the filets for lunch for all of us. After I dressed out the fish, I left the remains wrapped in a newspaper for disposal. Unbeknownst to me, our Laotian friend, Thongdy, picked up what remained of the fish carcass and brought it into the house where his wife, Sinsahk, cut up some vegetables and proceeded to cook what was left of the pike's skeleton in a large kettle. The fish soup which she served proved to be just as good as the main course. I can imagine that these people had learned to be very frugal during the time they spent in a Cambodian relocation camp, and they were not about to let anything go to waste . . . a little object lesson for us modern Americans.

Channel catfish

In northern Illinois channel catfish are ordinarily associated with muddy streams and rivers. In the past fifteen years, young channel catfish have become more readily available from commercial sources as fish for stocking northern ponds and lakes, although for many years this species has a history of use in pond and lake fishing in the south.

My pond has a lot of aquatic plants and the water can be regarded as somewhat clear (transparency over 36 inches) most of the time. For this reason, I felt the pond was not the best kind of habitat to be stocking channel cat.

In October of 1990, I decided to give this fish a try anyhow, and introduced 50 channel catfish from nine to twelve inches in length, which I had purchased from a commercial source. These fish were in good condition when stocked, so I had hopes of at least seeing some of them again at a later date. In March of 1991, I saw a sick channel cat swimming at the surface. A few bass had died this spring from what I presumed was pesticide runoff from the cornfield nearby. Dissolved oxygen had been adequate in the water all winter, so it was not a winterkill.

Late in May of 1991, I bought seven additional channel cat, averaging eight inches. Oddly, two of these fish were albinos which, I thought, might be easier to observe. I was wrong, as I never saw the albino catfish again, live or dead. Apparently, some predator also thought they were easy to observe.

In the following September of the same year, I did some fish sampling with a multi-mesh gill net. Although I caught bass, bluegills and one northern pike in the net, I saw no channel catfish. The next time I saw a catfish was a year later, when I found a 13 inch fish, floating dead with a hole in its head. Blue herons had been fishing in the pond regularly at that time of year, so I suspect that one of them had inflicted the wound.

Although there had been people fishing, both family and friends, none reported catching a catfish by the end of 1993, two years after the initial stocking. This lead me to believe that the survival of these fish had been very poor. In late October of 1993,

I caught a single, 15 inch channel cat in a gill net. The fish appeared to be in good condition. This is significant, because the fish had to survive a fish die-off which had occurred earlier in June, caused by low dissolved oxygen.

The next two times I saw channel catfish were in April and May of 1994. I observed one 15 inch fish that I collected in a gill net in April, and collected four additional catfish by electrofishing in May. Three of these were 15 to 16 inches in length, and one which was dead was 22 inches. I suspect we killed this latter individual with the electric shocker. With the exception of this fish, I returned to the water alive any other catfish I collected with a sampling device.

By the end of 1994, there was still no one who had caught a channel cat on hook and line. This was enough discouragement for me to discontinue thought of stocking any more of this species. However, in July of 1995, in amongst a number of larger fish that had been killed due to low dissolved oxygen, I found a single 17 inch channel cat. I'm fairly certain that this was the last, remaining catfish in the pond, as I have set nets since then and have caught neither channel catfish, nor any other larger fish.

It's too bad that channel cats hadn't taken well to my pond, because I would have liked to provide some spawning environment for them in the form of kegs or barrels, to see if they could reproduce. Maybe they'd surprise us like the northern pike did. In this instance, my first hunch was right . . . the pond doesn't provide a suitable habitat for channel catfish.

Trout

Trout are a cold water fish, and they also require higher concentrations of dissolved oxygen than most other fish species. About the only trout habitat on any scale in Illinois is Lake Michigan; otherwise, trout stocking and survival is only for the cold weather months (October to June). The few other bodies of water where I had observed trout survival in northern Illinois were deep, relatively infertile, borrow pits along the interstate highways, where the water stratified during the summer, providing a middle layer of water which was under 70°F; and had more than 5 mg/L of dissolved oxygen. Trout were able to survive in that rather confined area.

Figuring that trout would not live through the summer and to appease my own curiosity, I stocked three brown trout, averaging six inches, in May of 1965. I was able to see one of these fish alive in July, and to my surprise, once in awhile through the year I would see a fish feeding at the surface of the pond in the manner of a trout. One year later, in July of 1966, I found a large (17 inch) brown trout dead at the surface. This fish had made it for the fourteen months after stocking.

Somewhat encouraged, but still skeptical, I again stocked sixteen brown trout, four to eight inches in length, in early April of 1967. A week later we were able to capture two of these trout in a seine haul, along with a number of bluegills and bass. Another week later, I also stocked 16 rainbow trout, averaging ten inches, all in good condition. In June, a month after this, I found three dead trout, two browns and one rainbow. Just a week before, I had caught a 12 inch rainbow trout on hook and line. Its stomach was gorged with daphnia, a small invertebrate aquatic animal, plus a few damsel flies. During June, I continued to see trout actively feeding at the surface.

Water temperatures got very warm by August, from 74 to 84°F, but we could see no additional dead trout. No other trout were caught during 1967, except for a single rainbow which I captured in a seine haul in late September. This fish had grown to over 14 inches in length during the five months it was in the pond, and weighed about a pound. No trout were caught through the ice that following winter, even though considerable ice fishing was done, and no additional trout were ever seen again, live or dead.

My overview of our trout stocking experience was:
1. I wasn't surprised that most of the trout disappeared within a few weeks after stocking; however,
2. I *was* surprised that any trout made it through one whole summer of relatively high water temperatures.

It is possible that during warmer weather, a few trout may have been able to survive by swimming up into the underground ten inch diameter tile, which leads into the pond. Water seeping through this tile could have been cool enough to sustain the trout, during those periods when water temperatures were well above 70°F. A growing population of larger northern pike in our pond would also not enhance the survival of trout. I'm certain that a 20 inch northern would regard an eight to 12 inch trout as a delicate morsel.

The only circumstance where I would suggest stocking trout in a pond such as mine would be to introduce "catchable" size trout (over ten inches) early in the spring, then fish for them like crazy right into the summer when most or all will be expected to disappear. Don't expect any survival into the next year, although one or two oddballs might, just to prove me wrong.

Epilogue

Things One Might Learn from Having a Pond With Regard to Resource Management

Even if a person lives around a water detention pond, or a borrow pit in a suburban area, one is going to see elements of succession of aquatic life. Heavily "peopled" areas still will get their muskrats, ducks and geese, and invasion of various orders of aquatic plants. Last year I saw the endangered American bittern on the shore of Golfview Lake in the middle of Hinsdale, a large Chicago suburb. Water chemistry, although frequently inferior in densely populated areas, still follows certain limnological principles. It still freezes on top in the winter, becomes thermally stratified in the summer, and aquatic plant growth is still dependent upon water transparency.

An adult or a child living near a suburban pond can learn a lot about aquatic biology like his country cousin, although maybe not quite as much about actual resource management, because it is unlikely that the city slicker owns the entire watershed around the pond. Our two sons learned more about pond life than our two daughters, simply because they spent more time playing around the pond. As a boy, I used to sit on the front door steps of our suburban home and watch the cars splash through our perennial rain puddle on Jeanette Avenue, caused by a poorly functioning storm sewer. Besides enjoying this simple pastime, I learned that storm water leaves brown soil on the grass when it dries and that it does not smell too good. Also, the grass always ended up being greener there than on the rest of the lawn.

Listed below are some of the broad scale issues which a farm pond owner may confront:

I. Managing the watershed into the pond:
   A. Planting trees.
   B. Using soil protection techniques on cultivated land.
   C. Grass waterways.
   D. Conservation reserve.
   E. Assessing quality of water entering or leaving pond:
      1. Role of pond as a catchment basin.
      2. Impact of storms, runoff water and high winds on water quality.
   F. Impact on wildlife resources.
   G. Effects of pesticides and agricultural chemicals on life in the pond and the watershed.

II. Effects of pond and watershed on wells and ground water quality:
   A. Effects of agricultural or urban pesticides.
   B. Effects of other agricultural or urban chemicals.

And Finally

Since the last glacier covered this part of the midwest some 13,000 years ago, forming many bodies of open water, Mother Nature has been busy nudging these open waters back into wetlands of a different character. Our present day sloughs, marshes and organic deposits of muck and peat are legacies which give testament to this progression. Our own pond, just in the period of 33 years, has lost 15% of its open surface area to cattail growth and 10% of its volume to organic and inorganic bottom deposits. At this rate, by the time I'm 400 years old I'll be able to plant a garden where my pond used to be.

Of course, large, deep lakes, like Lake Geneva, will take thousands of years yet to become a wetland, but the process is going on, you can be certain. Since we replaced the Indians we have managed to accelerate the rate of filling and succession in most water bodies. This comes about by our endeavors at farming, highway construction and housing developements, all of which can increase erosion in the watersheds leading to lakes and ponds.

Epilogue

Management measures, like the initiation of conservation practices in the watersheds (no-till farming, grass waterways) and the removal of lake sediments by methods such as dredging, may slow the "lake to wetland" trend, but the trend *will* continue. Personally, I'm not too worried about it, I'll just wait for the next glacier. What about you?